T0157441

"STRONG MEDICINE" SPEAKS

ALSO BY AMY HILL HEARTH

Having Our Say: The Delany Sisters' First 100 Years
(with Sarah L. and A. Elizabeth Delany)

The Delany Sisters' Book of Everyday Wisdom
(with Sarah L. and A. Elizabeth Delany)

On My Own at 107: Reflections on Life Without Bessie
(with Sarah L. Delany)

*In a World Gone Mad: A Heroic Story of Love,
Faith, and Survival*
(with Norman and Amalie Petranker Salsitz)

The Delany Sisters Reach High

"STRONG MEDICINE" SPEAKS

A Native American Elder Has Her Say

An Oral History

Amy Hill Hearth

ATRIA BOOKS

NEW YORK   LONDON   TORONTO   SYDNEY

ATRIA BOOKS

A Division of Simon & Schuster, Inc.
1230 Avenue of the Americas
New York, NY 10020

First Atria Books hardcover edition March 2008

ATRIA BOOKS and colophon are trademarks of
Simon & Schuster, Inc.

For credits and permissions, see page 267.

For information about special discounts for bulk purchases,
please contact Simon & Schuster Special Sales at
1-800-456-6798 or business@simonandschuster.com.

Book text designed by Paul Dippolito

Manufactured in the United States of America

1   3   5   7   9   10   8   6   4   2

Library of Congress Cataloging-in-Publication Data

Hearth, Amy Hill, date.
"Strong Medicine" speaks : a Native American elder has
her say / Amy Hill Hearth.
p.   cm.
Includes bibliographical references.
1. Strong Medicine, 1922–   2. Delaware women—New Jersey—
Bridgeton—Biography. 3. Women shamans—New Jersey—Bridgeton—
Biography. 4. Delaware Indians—New Jersey—Bridgeton—Biography.
5. Delaware Indians—New Jersey—Bridgeton—History.
I. Strong Medicine, 1922–   II. Title.

E99.D2S775   2008
974.004'97345—dc22
[B]   2007020969

ISBN-13: 978-1-4767-8633-9
ISBN-10:   1-4767-8633-X

For Mark, Malaika, and Blair

Contents

Marion "Strong Medicine" Gould in the
front yard at her home.

Preface

This book is a rare look, from the inside, at contemporary Native American life as experienced by one tribe and, in particular, one important member of that tribe, a woman Elder named Strong Medicine.

It is unusual in several ways that are worth noting: it demolishes the Hollywood stereotype of the Native American woman as shy or passive; it focuses on a tribe from the East Coast, where Native Americans have played a pivotal role in the history of the United States but are too often overlooked in popular culture; and it was written, from the outset, with the input and approval of tribal leaders.

We live in a culture that ignores many voices. Insight, experience, and viewpoints are lost. The voices we do not hear often belong to people who are minority, female, and old. There are stories waiting to be told, and wisdom ready to be shared. When we laugh, cry, listen, and learn from others, the divisions between us begin to disappear.

Every book has a story behind it. The inspiration for this one comes from a Native American woman who lived long ago and about whom little is known. Her name was Mary, and she was born circa 1700. She married and had seven sons, some—perhaps all—patriots in the American Revolution. According to genealogical records, Mary was a Lenni-Lenape Indian, the same tribe of people to which Strong Medicine belongs.

Mary was my ancestor.

Until a few years ago, when my father came across information about Mary, I had assumed I was 100 percent white. My ancestors on my father's side came from England twelve generations ago, arriving in Massachusetts Bay Colony in 1635 and possibly earlier. Another branch of the family tree includes a rather famous tale of a Dutch woman who arrived in America at Sandy Hook, New Jersey, around 1640. (She arrived via shipwreck.) They sound like blue bloods, but in actuality they were a scrappy bunch—judging from early Colonial court records that detail their various transgressions, which include insulting Governor Peter Stuyvesant by claiming that he took bribes.

You couldn't ask for a more intriguing set of ancestors. Finding out about Mary, however, was especially tantalizing. As a journalist by training, my first instinct was to research the Lenni-Lenape Indians. Who were they? Where have they gone? Why do we not hear more about them?

Alas, my investigation would have to wait. At the time of my father's discovery I was fully preoccupied with my first book, *Having Our Say: The Delany Sisters' First 100 Years* (1993). An oral history of two sisters, the daughters of a man born into slavery, *Having Our Say* grew from a feature article I wrote for the *New York Times* in 1991.

Having Our Say turned out to be all-consuming in an unexpected but thoroughly delightful way. I had written it for the sake of history, knowing that if I didn't write the book, the stories would be lost forever. To my surprise (and to the amazement of the publishing industry, which had rather low expectations for it) *Having Our Say* was on the *New York Times* bestseller list for a total of two years.

I went on to write two more oral histories of the Delany sisters, in 1994 and 1997, and a children's book on them in 2003. In 1994–95, I worked on Broadway as an adviser on the theatrical adaptation of *Having Our Say*; in 1999 I was a consultant for the award-winning film adaptation. (Meanwhile, I also wrote *In a World Gone Mad: A Heroic Story of Love, Faith, and Survival*, an oral history of an elderly Jewish couple who escaped the Holocaust in Poland by posing as Christians and working for the Underground.)

Ten years passed before I was able to finally turn my attention full time to the Lenni-Lenape Indians. By that time I had accumulated three file drawers of newspaper clippings, books, and academic articles. I sat down to read them all.

While I was eager to explore my Native American ancestry, I was surprised and dismayed at the reaction of some acquaintances and professional colleagues who advised me not to "admit" (their word) to having Indian heritage.

"Why tell anyone?" asked one woman I'd known casually

for years. "You are white, you look white, no one would ever know." Several others responded, bizarrely, I thought, with jokes about savages and scalping, faux war whoops, and even imitations of Tonto (as in *The Lone Ranger*). These same people would not dream of making fun of other racial groups. I wondered what made them think it was okay to ridicule Native Americans.

As I began my research in depth, I was also dismayed at the uneven quality of material and conflicting information about Indians in general and the Lenni-Lenape in particular. Relying on my experience in investigative reporting, I decided to find the "real story."

There were so many false leads that I will provide only one example. In the spring of 2004, I was directed by a university-level research librarian to "Rankokus Indian Reservation" near Mount Holly, New Jersey. It is not, however, a reservation but rather Rancocas State Park, a land preserve leased in recent years to the Powhatan "Renape" Nation. When I visited in person, members of that tribe said they were descended from Powhatan Indians displaced from their native Virginia by the federal government. (Some of the members of that tribe in fact may have some Lenape ancestry, but the tribe is not predominantly Lenape.) The only Indian reservation in New Jersey was the Brotherton Reservation in Burlington County, which housed Lenni-Lenape families long ago. It was started in the mid-1700s but abandoned by 1802.

My research eventually led me to the Nanticoke Lenni-

Lenape Indians at the southernmost tip of New Jersey, near the great Delaware Bay. They are the largest and most organized Lenape tribe still living in the Land of the Ancestors, and, I believe, most closely related to my long-ago ancestor.

It is interesting to note that I was repeatedly warned by professionals (including a historian, a research librarian, and a journalist) that this tribe was notoriously reclusive and hostile to outsiders—and possibly would be that way even to a person with a Lenape ancestor. (I have since learned that the tribe's unofficial motto is "We are the friendliest people alive, but if someone messes with us they will live to regret it.")

I am not a naïve person. I assumed it would be difficult, perhaps impossible. I understood fully that they had been continually mistreated by the outside world, which I represented. I have a bad case of American "can-do" optimism, however, and figured it was worth a try.

In December 2004, I called Tribal Headquarters (the phone number is listed on the Internet). As luck would have it, the person who answered the phone was Tina "Little Wild Flower" Pierce Fragoso, a tribal historian and a Princeton- and Stanford-educated anthropologist. After a long phone conversation, she invited me to visit.

On the first Thursday of January 2005, I made the first of what would be many trips to Bridgeton, New Jersey, a two-and-a-half-hour drive from my home near New York City. I must have passed inspection, for I was invited back. I visited once more before being invited to attend my first tribal meeting, where I was asked to stand before the Tribal Council, state my name, and say why I was there. (At that point, I was not sure if I was there for personal reasons, or hoped to write an article or possibly even a book, which I explained to the Council.)

Having a Lenape ancestor was in my favor, but it was clear that earning their trust would take a long time. My approach was straightforward. I simply hung around as much as I dared, treated everyone with respect—and hoped that I'd grow on them.

A turning point came in April 2005. Members of the tribe went on a bus trip to visit the Smithsonian's newly opened National Museum of the American Indian in Washington, D.C. I was invited to come along (and even to bring my husband, Blair). After that, I was permitted to participate in the tribe's private Spiritual Gatherings, a rare invitation for an outsider.

It was at one of these Spiritual Gatherings, in May 2005, that I met an eighty-three-year-old woman Elder and matriarch of the tribe with the delightfully intriguing Indian name Strong Medicine. We were introduced by her son, the Chief of the tribe, at the Sacred Circle, prior to the beginning of a religious ceremony.

After the ceremony ended, the woman named Strong Medicine (her full name is Marion "Strong Medicine" Gould) allowed me to walk with her through the woods and back to the tented area where a meal was being prepared. At five feet six, she was taller than many of the other women, and physically very strong. She walked so quickly that I had to scramble to keep up with her.

A natural teacher, healer, and nurturer, she seemed to decide immediately to take me under her wing and teach me Lenape ways.

"See that? It's a weed, but it's edible," she said, pointing to a plant I had just stepped on. "Some Indians are ashamed to say they eat weeds, but I'm not! Why should I be? It's part of our culture."

And so I had my first dose of Strong Medicine.

I knew instantly that I wanted to talk to her further. Before long, I wanted to write an entire oral history. I envisioned it as similar in structure to *Having Our Say*. It would be her life story, in her own words, as well as her viewpoints, observations, and experiences. At the same time it would tell the larger story of the tribe itself and its unique place in American history.

I continued to attend tribal meetings and gatherings while working on the book. In fact, Chief Mark "Quiet Hawk" Gould added me to the agenda at tribal meetings so that I could provide updates on my progress. Prior to publication, Chief Gould reviewed this manuscript for accuracy, as did his brother, Billy Gould; the Reverend Dr. John "Smiling Thunderbear" Norwood, a Tribal Council member; and, of course, Marion "Strong Medicine" Gould herself.

A portion of the royalties from this book will go to the tribe. It was clear from the start, however, that members of the tribe did not expect remuneration and would have participated anyway. They were not motivated by money.

I conducted interviews, both formal (taped) and informal (notes), of dozens of members of the tribe, including the Chief, members of the Tribal Council, and numerous Elders and other members of the tribe. Many shared historical materials, documents, and photographs.

The primary focus, of course, is Marion Strong Medicine. This book is the result of hundreds of hours I have spent with her beginning in May 2005. I have written a narrative from thousands of anecdotes and stories that she shared with me. The words are all hers, but the order is mine.

Oral history, in its raw state, is almost unreadable due to the human tendency to repeat oneself, change the subject, interrupt one's own thought process with a diversion, and so on. I have taken the liberty, with Marion Strong Medicine's approval, of editing out such material.

It also should be noted that since the spoken word is more casual than the written word, readers will note the occasional use of slang, regional sentence structure, even occasional grammatical errors. It is these idiosyncracies, however, that give oral histories their authenticity and richness. Thus they have been left in place intentionally.

Section introductions, which I have written in my own "voice," are meant to provide context. Notes can be found at the end of the manuscript, along with a selected bibliography.

Creating this book has been an educational and spiritual journey, an opportunity to examine my life and values while

Preface

seeking information about a part of my heritage. While I can never know my long-ago Lenni-Lenape ancestor, Mary, I have been treated with great kindness and respect by her tribe and, in particular, by an extraordinary woman, a matriarch named Strong Medicine.

—*Amy Hill Hearth*

The official logo of the tribe features
a drawing of a turtle.

Introduction

They were the first Indian tribe in America to sign a treaty with the United States government. Their chiefs met with every major American figure from William Penn to George Washington.

They are the Lenni-Lenape, also called Delaware Indians, and contrary to what is frequently said of them today, they are not extinct. They are, in fact, alive and well, and eager to let the world know that.

For more than ten thousand years, their territory stretched from Manhattan Island to the Delaware Bay, including southeastern New York state, all of New Jersey, portions of eastern Pennsylvania (including what is now Philadelphia), and parts of Maryland and Delaware. Lenni-Lenape lands were unquestionably among the most magnificent in the world in terms of beauty and natural resources.

The Lenni-Lenape (LEN-ah La-NAH-pay), often called today simply "Lenape," are believed by many Native Americans to have been the first human beings on the East Coast of North America, predating all other Algonquin-speaking tribes. For this reason, they are known as the "Ancient Ones," the "Original People," or "Grandfather People."

They hunted and fished, built "longhouses" made of tree branches, bark, and animal skins, and grew crops they called "the three sisters"—variations of corn, beans, and squash. They honored the Creator, raised their families, and treated the treasures of nature with care and respect. No doubt they thought it would go on like that forever.

But then the invaders came.

It began, for the Lenape, on a spring day in 1524, when a strange-looking ship—a great waterfowl, they apparently thought, or perhaps the Creator himself—suddenly appeared in the waters between what is now called Brooklyn and Staten Island, New York. The captain was the European explorer Giovanni da Verrazzano, an Italian sailing a French vessel, *La Dauphine*. Verrazzano would recall later that the Lenape, "clad with feathers of fowls of diverse colors," paddled out to greet him, making "great shouts of admiration."

This dramatic event occurred more than eighty years *before* the English founded the ill-fated Jamestown settlement in Virginia, where the famous story of Pocahontas unfolded; and a century prior to the arrival of the Pilgrims, in 1620, at what would become the Plymouth Colony in Massachusetts, site of the first Thanksgiving.

After Verrazzano's encounter, it was not long before other white men appeared on Lenape shores. Explorers from Italy, France, Portugal, and England competed to be first to claim the land as their own. In another pivotal moment, Henry Hudson, in 1609, sailed into New York's harbor and explored the river that would one day be named for him. (Often left out of the history books is that in September of that year alone, thirteen Lenape were shot by Hudson's men in different incidents.)

The explorers called the native people "Indians," a term coined in the fifteenth century in a bout of wishful thinking by a lost Christopher Columbus, who had been hoping to find a passage to the Far East when he was actually in the Caribbean. The designation, although wildly incorrect, became part of the lexicon (and is still used, even today, by some native peoples, including many of the Lenape).

Explorers to the region were soon followed by Dutch and English settlers, who began referring to the Lenape as "Delaware Indians," a name derived from Baron De La Warr, an Englishman. Time and again, the settlers cheated, lied to, and committed genocide against indigenous people. An untold number of Indians also died of diseases, such as smallpox and measles, to which they had no immunity.

Tragically, the abusive and murderous tactics used against the East Coast tribes—called "Nations of First Contact" by Native Americans—would become the template for the way other tribes would be treated in the coming years as white settlers moved ever westward.

The Lenape, in particular, seemed to be in the crossfire. As luck would have it, their lands were especially coveted. Their leaders were thrust into a world they did not understand. It was the Lenape who famously "sold" Manhattan Island for the equivalent of twenty-four dollars to the Dutchman Peter Minuit in 1626. (Historians now believe that the Lenape probably thought they were "renting" or sharing a small portion of the island.)

William Penn, founder of Philadelphia, behaved more honorably. Penn's treaties with the Lenape were more equitable and, at least during his lifetime, they were upheld. Also fair-minded were the Swedes, who started a small settlement known as New Sweden. They were, however, the exceptions.

The presence of the European invaders inevitably created chaos among (and within) individual tribes, undermining and interfering with traditional Indian alliances. The native people soon became entangled in the power struggles and wars of the white man.

More often than not, the Lenape sided with American colonists. "They served as scouts for Roger's Rangers in the French and Indian War; received commendations from

Engraving showing the sale of Manhattan Island.

4

George Washington for their heroism during the American Revolution; signed the first Indian treaty of alliance with the fledgling United States in 1778; joined the United States Army fighting Florida's Indians in the Second Seminole War in the 1830s; and aided the Americans during the Mexican War," writes Evan T. Pritchard, a professor of Native American history at Marist College in Poughkeepsie, New York, in his book, *Native New Yorkers: The Legacy of the Algonquin People of New York*.

The Lenape arguably suffered more than any other indigenous people in North America. "No other tribe on the Continent has been so much moved and jostled about by civilized invasions," wrote the nineteenth-century American artist George Catlin.

Yet the general public seems to know little of them. For example, New York City has so efficiently wiped out any memory of the Lenape that Pritchard says it should be called "City of Amnesia."

Much of what has been written about them during the past four hundred years is misleading or simply wrong, according to the Lenape. Most egregious is that they are often referred to as a "lost" tribe. Even in the summer of 2005, a major American newspaper referred to them as if they were a relic of the past, like dinosaur bones in a museum.

The facts are far different. "Descendants of New York City Lenape were removed by treaty at least twenty times and sent to Oklahoma, Ontario, and Wisconsin, where they were subject to poverty, disease, and death," Pritchard writes. "The exodus of these real Native New Yorkers was one of the greatest tragedies in U.S. history."

Today the largest populations of Lenape live on reservations at Bartlesville and Anadarko, Oklahoma; and at Six Nations, Moraviantown, and Muncy Town in Ontario. Others live in Kansas, Colorado, Ohio, and Wisconsin.

What is truly surprising and impressive is that a small number managed to stay on their ancestral lands. These tribes live in Pennsylvania, Delaware, and New Jersey. The largest and most vibrant is the Nanticoke Lenni-Lenape, led by Chief Mark "Quiet Hawk" Gould in Bridgeton, New Jersey. His tribe counts more than 2,800 members. New genealogical research, enabled by the Internet, indicates that as many as five thousand people are eligible to enroll as tribal citizens. (Enrollment eligibility is based on having a minimum of one-quarter Nanticoke or Lenape ancestry from historically documented core tribal family lines.)

The tribe's name reflects a historic, close kinship with a tribe of Nanticoke, or "Tidewater People," who live in Delaware and at the Maryland seashore. Members of the tribe are mostly Lenape, but Nanticoke ancestry is not uncommon as well. Among the women Elders is the Chief's mother, Marion "Strong Medicine" Gould, who helped the ancient tribe reorganize itself into a modern entity in the 1970s. Her Lenape ancestry, along with her late husband's, extends to the earliest known families in the tribe.

That at least some of the Lenape were not displaced, and are not housed on a reservation, is an enormous victory over fate. The connection to one's ancestral land is a defining part of Native American culture. Luther Standing Bear, a Lakota, has written that white people do not comprehend the depth of this connection. "The man from Europe is still a foreigner and an alien," he writes. "But in the Indian the spirit of the land is still vested."

Described by other Indian tribes as peacemakers and by European colonists as fair-minded, the Lenape have another characteristic that is clear to those who meet them and study their history. They are tenacious survivors in a world that, even now, often denies their existence. How they managed is an untold story.

PART I

The Hidden People

O N A LATE SPRING afternoon, as the sun nears its highest point, fifty men and women form a large circle in the middle of a field, deep in the woodlands and marshes that border a great river. Each one stands quietly, focused on a small, smoky bonfire that smells of sage and tobacco. There is a chill in the air from a morning rain shower, and both the fire and the rays of the sun are welcome.

The fire crackles and hisses. It takes center stage until the sudden, piercing declarations of a mockingbird reverberate from the upper branches of a nearby tree. The people turn their heads in response, instinctively, and listen. Several of the Elders smile and nod their heads. They are amused by the bird's bossiness, and admire its courage.

The night before, many of the young people—and even a few Elders—had stayed up all night to dance and drum in the moonlight. Voices singing traditional songs had carried through the cool night air. After a while, in that environment, the concept of time began to disappear. Was it 2005? Or several millennia ago, or perhaps some date in between?

The previous night's celebrations welcomed the spring,

but today's ceremony is most important of all. It is here that they will pray to the Creator.

The last member of the Tribal Council finally arrives, and the ceremony begins. All eyes are on Chief Mark "Quiet Hawk" Gould and his eighty-three-year-old mother, Marion "Strong Medicine" Gould. Less than forty-eight hours earlier, the Chief's father—Strong Medicine's husband of almost sixty-five years—died after a long illness and with his family by his side. The ceremony in the Sacred Circle, always an intensely spiritual experience for the members of the tribe, will be especially poignant this day.

Strong Medicine sits quietly in a chair, one of several placed in the circle for Elders. Her posture is ramrod-straight, and her feet are crossed, ladylike, at the ankles. The sun reflects off her shoulder-length silver hair. She wears a gray cardigan sweater, and a long plaid skirt.

The Chief speaks. He reminds everyone that the ceremony is sacred. Each person will have a chance to pray and sprinkle tobacco—a gift to the Creator—into the fire. The Chief nods to Lewis "Gray Squirrel" Pierce, a Spiritual Leader and cochairman of the tribe, who will orchestrate the ceremony. Gray Squirrel notes that prayers should be said for others, not for oneself, and that each person, after praying, should walk once around the fire before returning to the same place in the circle.

One at a time they move toward the fire, pausing to collect a few dried tobacco leaves from Gray Squirrel. Some kneel by the fire and take a long time; others toss the leaves into the flames more quickly. For each person it is a solitary moment.

Soon it is Strong Medicine's turn to pray. The Chief gently extends his hand, and, taking it, she rises from the chair. They walk toward the fire, the son protective and respectful, the mother strong and steady. He does not let go of her arm, even as they approach Gray Squirrel.

With dried tobacco leaves in hand, she is ready to pray. As Gray Squirrel watches, the Chief escorts his mother closer to the fire. Suddenly, he stops and stands aside. She will take the last steps alone.

As she kneels to pray, her lips moving silently, some avert their eyes but others watch sympathetically. Scattering the tobacco leaves into the flames, the fire speaks back, spitting and hissing, and for a moment she disappears behind a veil of smoke. She lingers. No one in the prayer circle moves, not even a few small children who clutch their mothers' long skirts. The moment belongs to her. At last she rises, walks purposefully around the fire once, and takes her son's arm again, allowing him to escort her back to her place in the circle.

Marion Strong Medicine has just said good-bye to her husband. It is the same way in which the women of her tribe have been letting go of their loved ones, perhaps even on this same grassy field, for more than ten thousand years.

Marion Strong Medicine (Marion Purnell)
in her high school yearbook picture, 1940.

1

I was fourteen years old the first time I set eyes on my husband. I knew he was the man I was going to marry someday, and I did, when I was eighteen and he was twenty.

I was born Marion Doris Purnell on April 25, 1922, but my Indian name is "Strong Medicine." I was given that name about thirty years ago because I know a thing or two about plants and herbs, and because it suits my personality—or so I'm told. People have come to me for advice, all of my life. They know I will give it to 'em straight!

I was born in Bridgeton, New Jersey, and I have lived nearly all my life here, on the same stretch of road. It's in the southern part of New Jersey, near the Delaware Bay. Most people don't even know this part of New Jersey exists. It's beautiful country, mostly farmland and marshes.

When my husband and I were coming up, our tribe was in hiding. We were a hidden people. You wouldn't have been able to tell because we went about our lives like other people. We dressed like white people, we had "normal" jobs, we went to church.

But we were Indian.

Even today, you probably would not recognize us because

15

we wear regular clothing, live in houses, drive cars, and eat the same kinds of foods you do. We do not live on a reservation, and only at Powwows and tribal gatherings, or for special occasions, do we put on our feather headdresses, beaded clothing, moccasins, and face paint in remembrance of early life.

Of course, there are other differences. We live the Indian way, and always have. We have reverence for God and all living things. We are a very tight-knit group, and we help each other. We revere our children and our Elders. We don't live for the moment, the way many Americans do, and we are not as likely to be motivated by material things or by money. Integrity and honesty are extremely important to us.

Many white people have a very rigid idea of who Indians are. There is no "typical" Indian any more than there is a "typical" black person or "typical" Jewish person. But when people think of Indians, they think of the stereotype of the Plains Indians, riding horses and hunting buffalo. You know, the guys who killed Custer. They think we all live on a reservation somewhere. Well, it's simply not so. It's not really their fault for thinking that, though. There are so few books out there that tell the true story of Indians. Some of it's our fault because we don't like to talk to outsiders, so it's hard for people to get good, first-hand information. As for the movies, well, I will share my opinion about that later.

It's important that people understand that not all tribes are alike, nor do we look alike. Many of us, especially on the East Coast, have some ancestry other than Indian. That's because in the East we've been coexisting with white people—and black people, too—for almost four hundred years.

The Hidden People

My mother, for example, was Lenape with a little white blood. My father was Indian, too, on his mother's side, but he was also part black. His great-grandmother was a slave in Maryland. If you look at my family tree, it's very complicated in terms of race. But I'm more Lenape Indian than anything else. And that's how I was raised.

My husband's name was Wilbert Gould, though most people knew him as "Wilbur Junior." His Indian name was "Wise Fox." He was Lenape but he had a small amount of white blood—Irish. He had blue eyes!

People will say to your face, "Well, you can't be Indian if you have blue eyes" or "So-and-so's not Indian. He looks black, so he must be black!" People can be downright rude about it. We're a little tired of people trying to tell us who we are. Another thing we hear all the time is, "But there aren't any Indians in New York and New Jersey." Or they'll say we are extinct.

Mercy.

Maybe they think there was no one living here but rabbits and squirrels before white people got here and "discovered" the land. The truth is, we've been killed off, moved around, and more or less treated very badly for four hundred years.

What happened to another tribe—the Cherokee—is fairly well known. They were marched out west by U.S. soldiers to a reservation, and a lot of them died along the way. They called it the Trail of Tears.

What most people don't realize is that this happened to a lot of tribes. It happened to my tribe. There's a story told in our tribe that the last trainload of Lenape were sent out west to a reservation in 1924, when I was two years old. So you see why we kept quiet. We kept quiet in order to survive.

Being Indian was a secret, something you didn't talk about outside the family. If the government came around and asked questions, like when they did the census, the members of our tribe might not talk to them. Sometimes we would say we were "colored." That's a term they used in the old days for people who are not white. Well, the government workers were white and they didn't know what the heck we were. They thought we meant we were "black" when we said "colored." We let them think that. I tell you what, the United States census must be messed up, going way, way back, 'cause I'm pretty sure we aren't the only ones who did that.

See, you were better off being black than Indian. The government didn't take your home and land and make you go out west to a reservation if you were black. But they did that to Indians. They did it all the time.

Until four hundred years ago, when the white people came, Lenape land included Manhattan Island, New Jersey, and part of Pennsylvania, too, including Philadelphia. Hmmm. Maybe they should give it all back. Ha!

Now, I think that's funny. That's my type of humor. Hey, you have to laugh at yourself and things that go on around you. There are plenty of things that can make you sad, crazy, or angry, so you better find ways to enjoy this life. That is the secret of living well.

2

My role in the tribe, as one of the Elders, is to be part of the backbone, so to speak. Of course, if I really disagree with my son, he'll be hearing about it. My son is the Chief of the tribe, and has been for a long time. I just wait until he comes by my house so I don't tangle with him in front of the rest of the tribe, that's all. He may be the Chief, but I'm still his mother!

It's part of our tribe's culture for the women to be boss. We are a matriarchal society. Even though my son is the Chief, he has to listen to what the women have to say. He is used to it because he grew up with it.

Historically, Lenape women were very powerful, much more so than the white women who came to America. Our men couldn't go to war without the women's approval. If the women thought it was a bad idea, the men didn't go.

I was brought up the Indian way, and sometimes I just feel totally out of sync with the world around me. I look around and I'm thinking, Hey, why are people building these huge houses? Why do they live the way they do? They just come in with bull-dozers, they don't care. They take down the trees and put in grass and then they have to water it, and they put all these chemicals down on top of it, and all that stuff runs into the marsh. I'm worried that we are going to run out of clean drinking water.

When I pick up a newspaper today or turn on the television, most of the bad stuff I see is caused by greed. All anybody ever thinks about is money. I don't have any money, and I never have. And you know what? I really don't care. I could care less! I am doing just fine with what I have. The only thing that's important to me, as far as money is concerned, is to keep my burial fund paid up. I want to have a proper funeral when the time comes, and I don't want my sons to have to pay for it.

I am perfectly happy in my bungalow. I wouldn't be any happier in some great big mansion. Especially if I had to drive two hours to a job, which is what a lot of folks seem to be doing. They're wasting all that gasoline, and then they're mad at the world because they're stuck in traffic! They build a house that's nowhere near anything, and it's so big I bet they're all in different rooms and not even talking to each other anyway. It don't make any sense! If someone was to give me a mansion in the suburbs, I'd give it back.

You don't need money to live well. Most folks don't know that, though. They think you're a fool if you don't worship money. The Indian way, traditionally, is very different. What we care about is family ties, and our community. It's like food and water to us. We don't have fancy cars and all. But we got each other. We know where we belong. We know where home is.

It's the way we view the world and our place in it. Most importantly, we respect the natural world. To Indians, the earth is "Mother" and the sky is "Father."

The Hidden People

When I was coming up, I learned a lot about nature from my mother and her sister, my aunt Mary. Every Saturday, we used to walk down to Aunt Mary's house, a couple of miles down the road. And then from there, we walked another mile or two. We used to go arbutus hunting, back in the woods. I don't think there's any arbutus left in the world! I haven't seen any recently, anywhere. They weren't very pretty, just little flowers that grow on the ground. But oh, they did smell so good.

Mom and Aunt Mary would tell us to be very careful with the plants. If the plants weren't thick enough for us to pick, Mom would say, "Don't touch 'em, there's not enough of them to go around."

We had a wagon, and my little brother and sister would get tired and climb in it, and I'd end up having to pull it. It was a dirt road, so what few cars went by, you'd have a cloud of dust.

I'll tell you what really kills me: these people in big business and the government who insist there's no global warming going on. I read in the newspaper that the polar ice caps are melting. Whoa! Now, that's some scary stuff. We should listen to the scientists! And the old-timers like me! What is it going to take for some people to believe that there's global warming, and to do something about it? I guess someday they'll wake up and there'll be a polar bear sitting on their front step. I guess that's when they'll believe it. Ha!

I wonder if people in power care about their children or grandchildren. I know that's harsh, but I think it's a fair question. They are not thinking of the future! The Indian way is to try to make decisions based on how it might affect seven generations from the present. Indians are thinking about the future while everybody else today is living for the moment.

Another thing that worries me is all these kids sitting around on their rear ends today. They just sit and stare at the television, and they're getting fat. Or they play those video games. They need to get off their tails and get outside and play! I wonder if these kids are going to even know what nature is, sitting in their big houses with air-conditioning, staring at a TV screen. Somebody needs to teach them about nature. It is a gift from the Creator.

I like to wake up to the sound of birds singing outside my window. It makes me start my day right. Why, I even talk to some of the birds. There's one that sits way up in the tree, I can't even see him when I'm outside. He and I, we have conversations. I say something to him, like "Good morning, bird," and he answers me. I'm serious! That bird talks back to me. I have no idea what he's saying, but on some level we're communicating. I get a kick out of that kind of thing. That's what makes life grand.

PART II

In the Land of the Ancestors

WHEN VISITING the home of Marion "Strong Medicine" Gould, one of the first things that draws the eye is a cluster of family portraits carefully arranged on a shelf and another grouping affixed to the wall behind it. In the back row of the shelf, peering out from the rear, is the likeness of a woman who appears white, her face framed by an elegant, nineteenth-century collar.

This woman was Strong Medicine's grandmother, a daughter of a German woman who hailed from Pennsylvania Dutch country and a man who was a full-blooded Lenape Indian. There are many other threads of Lenape ancestry in Strong Medicine's lineage, with the result that she is predominantly Lenape.

The tribe's heritage is unusually complex, even among East Coast tribes. A small segment of the Lenape can trace its lineage to the British royal family, owing to a single colonist with ties to the throne who came to America and fathered several children with a Lenape woman.

Still others have some Swedish ancestry dating to the 1600s, when a group of colonists formed "New Sweden" in

Lenape territory near Philadelphia. Members of the Swedish government and royal family visit occasionally, and Sweden even considers the tribe to be a sovereign nation.

It is a complicated and little-known part of American history. What all the members of the tribe have in common, however, is a significant portion of Lenape ancestry, and perhaps some Nanticoke as well.

While the Lenape are often said to belong to one of three branches—Munsee, in the northern region; Unami, in the southern region; and Unalachtigo, thought to live inland—at least one anthropologist, the late Herbert C. Kraft, argued that these divisions never existed. Instead, he suggested that newly arrived Europeans misunderstood Lenape culture and language, and assigned geographic divisions.

The Lenape, meanwhile, have their own way of viewing themselves: the wolf clan, which is people who traditionally live in the mountains; the turkey clan, or people who live inland; and the turtle clan, who live along rivers and the sea, as Marion Strong Medicine's tribe does. The Lenape do use the terms *Munsee* and *Unami,* but in reference to various dialects of their language, which is said to be one of the most complex on earth.

If you ask Marion Strong Medicine about her ancestors, she mentions that her mother grew up in Burden's Hill, a few miles down a two-lane road in Salem County near where her son, the Chief, lives today. She points up and down the road in front of her bungalow—"over here" and "over there"—to describe where her parents, grandparents, and great-grandparents lived. The same is true for her late husband's ancestors. No one seems to have gone very far. Her eldest son, for example, lives next door.

That, however, is part of what Marion Strong Medicine calls "the Indian way." The connection to the land—and to one another—is so powerful that only a few leave, and those who do are often reluctant to do so. The pursuit of jobs, education, and other opportunities sometimes lures younger members of the tribe, but many try to return "home" eventually.

Driving around the area, a visitor could get lost easily. Strong Medicine, and many other members of the tribe, have a penchant for referring to places that aren't on any official map.

Gouldtown, for example, is on most state maps but not all. It's a tiny town nearby that was named for Strong Medicine's husband's family. When Wilbur "Wise Fox" Gould was growing up, he attended Gouldtown School and many of his family members attended Gouldtown (Methodist) Church. His final resting place is at Gouldtown Cemetery.

Then, there is the place the Elders call "Fordville." A Methodist church there is routinely referred to as "the Indian Church" or "Fordville Church" although, as it turns out, its actual name is St. John's. In neighboring Salem County, "Burden's Hill" is also missing from the official lexicon.

It seems the best thing to do is to ask Strong Medicine to come along for a ride and serve as tour guide. She agrees cheerfully, and off we go. We're off to a bad start, however, when she refers to "the Pike," and I assume she is referring to the New Jersey Turnpike, which is many miles away. The mystery is solved when she reveals that her "Pike" is a name from long ago for a two-lane road that connects the small cities of Bridgeton and Millville.

We drive all over. We pay no attention to the clock in the car, deciding that we'll follow "Indian time" instead. Roughly translated, "Indian time" means "We'll get there when we get there."

She takes me to the cemetery where her husband is buried, and to a different cemetery that is her parents' final resting place. She shows me the library, greatly expanded, where she spent many happy hours as a girl. She shows me the house where she grew up, and the house where one of her mother's sisters lived. We see the high school, now a junior high, from which she graduated in 1940. Nearby is the street where her grandparents lived. Their house is long gone, torn down and replaced by a store. Much of the little city of Bridgeton has changed from its heyday, and not all the changes are for the better. The manufacturing jobs, from sewing factories to catsup producers, are long gone.

Strong Medicine is a backseat driver. "Are we going to sit here and wait all day?" she teases me when I miss several opportunities to make a left turn. But I am cautious. After all, I have some precious cargo—the Chief's mother—in my car.

In the countryside, the farms thrive, seemingly un-changed. Many are still owned by the same families. "That's Mood's," she says, pointing out one family farm near Mullica Hill, a town known for its antiques dealers. "We used to come up here, long, long time ago, and buy fruit."

You can still buy fruit at Mood's, at a roadside stand. If you have the time and inclination, you can even borrow a bucket and pick your own blueberries for a modest price. While blueberries are a local specialty, many other crops grow well here, too, among them Jersey tomatoes, sweet corn, peaches, cherries, wheat, soybeans, sod, and even delicate ornamental trees and bushes. This year has been a particularly bountiful one for peaches. At one farm, a homemade ladder rests invitingly against a peach tree, and a hand-drawn sign welcomes passersby to stop. "Too Many Peaches," it reads, almost pleadingly. "Help Yourself!"

It is no wonder that European explorers coveted Lenape land. In addition to rich soil for farming, Lenape territory included immense forests, two great rivers—the Delaware and the Hudson—and even the spectacular harbor of New York, often said to be the greatest natural harbor in the world. That any of Strong Medicine's tribe are still here is a remarkable feat.

3

I consider myself lucky to be living in the land of my ancestors and not on a government reservation far away. The connection to the land is very strong for Indian people. To us, it isn't where we live, it's who we are.

I know I am walking the same piece of earth that my ancestors did, going back ten thousand years. I know their bones have turned to dust under my feet and someday, mine will, too. It's the natural order of things.

The members of my tribe are part of a huge extended family living mostly in two counties—Salem and Cumberland. My mother came from a clan that lived at Burden's Hill, near Quentin, in Salem County. Her name was Mildred Eldora Pierce Purnell, but she was called Millie.

On Burden's Hill, where Mom came from, people were all mixed up, race-wise, but mainly Lenape Indian. They were all shades. Nearly everybody had some white ancestry because of intermarriage. Hey, white people have been in this area for four centuries—it's going to happen. My great-grandmother, for example, was a German lady. She was from Pennsylvania Dutch country. She married a full-blooded Lenape Indian man who went by the name of Jones. When

Millie Pierce Purnell (SEATED), Marion
"Strong Medicine" Gould's mother;
and her mother's aunt Clara, circa 1916.

*they had children, some of them looked Indian, some of them
didn't.*

*There was one great-aunt of mine who was said to have had
a ruddy complexion. She wasn't real dark. But she had brothers who really looked Indian, like Uncle Frank, who had long
straight dark hair. It was so long he could sit on it. He used to
wear a big, wide-brimmed hat whenever he went anywhere
with his horse and wagon.*

So my mother's mother was half Indian. She married a Pierce, and my mother was among their children. The Pierces were pretty much all Lenni-Lenape blood. Thus my mother was mostly Lenape, from two different families—the Joneses and the Pierces.

My mother was the oldest of three sisters. They were a threesome that did everything together. They were three M's—Millie, Mary, and Mabel. There were two brothers, too. I remember, when I was about three, my uncle George got in trouble with Grandmom because he took me sledding in a field with barbed wire in it. Oh, Grandmom chewed him out good.

Grandmom's house had ghosts in it, but nobody worried

Mamie Purnell, Marion "Strong Medicine"
Gould's paternal grandmother, circa 1920s.

Grandpa Pierce, Marion "Strong Medicine"
Gould's maternal grandfather, who loved to
tell ghost stories, outside his wood-frame
house, circa 1930s.

*about it one bit. Those houses on Burden's Hill, all on one side
when you're heading toward Bridgeton, they were all "funny."
That whole area is haunted.*

*My mother and my aunts would be in one room, say the
kitchen. They'd be snapping beans or something like that. And
a framed photograph would fall off the wall. That happened a
lot, and the glass never broke. That's when they knew the spirit
of that person—one of the ancestors—was in the room. The
ghost would follow the three of them from room to room. I was
very tiny but I remember them all talking about it. And my*

Ella Jones Pierce, Marion "Strong Medicine"
Gould's maternal grandmother, circa 1890s.

*aunts and my mother would say to me, "Don't worry, Marion,
it's just the ghost." They were very low-key about it. When you
live with a ghost your whole life—when you grow up with it
like Mom and Aunt Mary and Aunt Mabel did—it doesn't
bother you. You just get used to it.*

*Another sign that the ghost was moving around Grand-
mom's house was when the door would suddenly open and no
one was there. This happened a lot, too. The front door had a
latch. Nobody had locks. The three sisters would be sitting
there, doing beadwork or something like that, and the latch*

would pop up and the door would creak open. Somebody would say, "Oh, there's the ghost again."

Grandpa Pierce was always telling ghost stories. Even after we moved to Bridgeton, a few miles away, he would get in his car and come down for a visit and scare us children half to death with his ghost stories. We didn't have electricity, not upstairs, anyway. When it came time to go to bed, we had to take these flickering lanterns up the stairs, which made Grandpa's stories even scarier.

A lot of people who lived out here, outside of Bridgeton, were high-yaller Indian. By that I mean they were not real dark. Their skin had a yellowish tone to it. When I use the term high yaller, I mean anyone of that color, whether they're black or Indian. Lots of times white people lumped us into the same category. They called us "colored." We often went along with it because we didn't want them to know we were Indian.

I guess everyone pretty much knows that black people, when they could, sometimes tried to pass for white. This was true with Indians, too! There were Indian people around here who left their families and went to Philadelphia and places like that, and lived as white people. You had families that split up—some people passed, and some didn't, in the same family. They went their separate ways.

I remember the first time I learned that you can't tell what people are, necessarily, just by looking at 'em. I guess I was about twelve or thirteen years old. Sometimes we used to take a bus into Bridgeton. One time, my cousin Betty and I were getting on the bus and we saw this lady who had these cotton stockings that wouldn't stay up. I don't know why things like that seem so funny to you when you're that age, but we thought it was hilarious. There was this little short lady—she had blond hair and blue eyes and everything—and the only thing we could see were those stockings crawling back down her legs. Betty and I found our seats while Mom got on the bus behind us. The woman with the sagging stockings was sitting in the opposite seat, and when she saw my mother she said, "Hi, Cousin Millie!"

I was shocked. Believe me, I had no idea this lady was kin to my mother. So you see, my mother's family was every kind of color, even though they were more Indian than anything else. And I made up my mind right then and there not to judge people by the color of their skin or anything else.

My mother, in fact, could have passed for white if she had wanted to. I mean, she wouldn't have fooled Indian people—they would have known—but she could have fooled white people. Mom had a golden opportunity, you might say, to live white but she turned it down. When she was real young, she was working in the house of a white lady named Mrs. Fogg in Salem County. This lady tried to get Mom to marry a white man who worked on her property, but Mom said no, and Mrs. Fogg got mad. She really thought Mom should marry white to improve her place in the world.

I'm not going to judge people, Indian or black, who passed for white, because their lives were so much more pleasant as white people. I can't say I admire it but I don't think you can put people down for it.

Well, Mom decided to have none of that. She was Indian,

Millie Pierce Purnell, Marion "Strong Medicine"
Gould's mother, in Indian dress outside the house
where she grew up in Burden's Hill, circa 1914.

*and that was that. But this meant she had to leave Mrs. Fogg's
house and get another job and a new place to live. So she went
to Bridgeton, in Cumberland County, where she got a job
working for a family that owned the dye house. She worked in
their home, and somewhere along the line she met my father,
who was born and raised in Bridgeton.*

*Now, my daddy's name was William H. Purnell Jr. Daddy
was a dark-skinned man. I was told his mother was Indian
with some Negro ancestry. His father also had a black ancestor—down in Maryland, in the Eastern Shore region—who
was a slave and had at least one child by the white slave owner,
but it was never clear to me if that child was my great-*

Marion "Strong Medicine" Gould's
father, William Purnell, with his dog,
Bobby, circa 1930s.

grandfather or one of his brothers or sisters. People didn't talk about stuff like that when I was coming up.

I was only three, but I remember my great-grandfather. I remember sitting on his knee and he would talk to me. He was a tall man, or so it seemed to me. The funny thing was, he was a big man but his kids—the ones I knew, anyway—were all very short. He was way, way taller than his daughter, who kept house for him.

A lot of that side of the family eventually settled further north of here. They moved for the simple reason that there was more opportunity for people of color elsewhere.

Now, my father's father, I called him Grandpop. His name was William Purnell. He was one of those kind of people who would sit back and smoke his cigar and read his Bible and whatnot. Or else he would go out and work in the yard. He was a quiet person. He'd had a good job working for the railroad. He was the head of a group of men that went around to see that there's nothing on the railroad tracks, to make sure the trains wouldn't derail. The train tracks went straight through town, so sometimes on my way to school I would see him and his crew going by on a handcar, one of those old-timey railroad cars that you moved along by pumping a handle up and down. If he saw me he would shout my name and wave.

Marion "Strong Medicine" Gould's mother, Millie Pierce Purnell (CENTER), and Millie's two sisters, Mary (LEFT) and Mabel (RIGHT), in the 1930s.

Grandpop worked for the railroad until he was, oh, probably eighty years old or more. He had another job, too. He would walk from his house out to the cemetery a mile or so away. He would go out there and take care of the cemetery, make sure the grass was cut. There was another old man that went with him. I guess it kept them healthy, all that walking and mowing.

My father's mother was also part Indian. Her name was Marie, but everybody called her Mamie. She used to say, "Marion, if you don't feel right, if you don't feel good, just go outside. Take care of your flower bed and forget about everything else. If it's wintertime, go dig yourself a path in the snow whether you need it or not. You don't have to think too much to plant anything or scoop snow, and your mind can go back and figure out what's wrong." I still take her advice to this day.

They lived in Bridgeton across from the old high school. The house is gone now, torn down. Grandpop lived until his late eighties, and Grandmother did, too. But she died before he did. She had cancer for years and she never had an operation or treatment. My father was second oldest of their children, and all that's left living from that generation is one brother—one of my uncles.

Now my generation is getting up there in years. I'm eighty-three years old, my sons are in their sixties. I like to tease my sons and say, "Hey, you're not spring chickens anymore!" But no matter how old they get, they're still my little boys.

4

I was my parents' second child. The first one, a boy born in 1921 or thereabouts, died from crib death, or some kind of apnea. Whatever it was, I don't know much about it because Mom never did talk about it.

I was born the following year, on the twenty-fifth of April, 1922. I was born at home, delivered by a white woman doctor—a Doctor Bacon—and her nurse. Everybody in town

Baby Marion, circa 1923.

knew them. When I was a girl I'd see them driving around in a Model T, and she always carried one of those old-timey black bags that doctors used to have.

Mom didn't give me any details about my birth, other than that I was a big baby. I always had the idea that she and Daddy were very happy to have me, after losing that first baby. Certainly, I felt loved from my earliest days.

After they had me, Mom got pregnant again but it didn't go well. All her hair fell out, though it grew back later. The baby—another boy—was born alive but he didn't live. I don't really know what the problem was with Mom, if something was wrong inside of her or if those two babies were weak in some way. At any rate, Mom and Daddy did have two more children, after me, that lived. My brother, Boyer, who was born September 7, 1926, and my sister, Dianne, on May 28, 1929.

So I was the big sister. There were three of us, which was a small family in those days. I felt like I always had to do more than my share because I was the oldest. Boyer was four years younger, and Dianne was seven years younger, so I was put in charge of them a lot of the time.

At the same time, I knew what it was like to be treated like a little sister because my father was second oldest of a big clan, and his youngest brother and sister were just a few years older than me. Uncle Boyer (my brother was named after him) and Aunt Alice used to give me fits. They'd tease me and boss me around. Even when we all got older, they treated me like a little sister.

Looking back now, I think I always knew we were Indian.

I remember when my mom told us, and it wasn't news to me. I knew from the way we looked and where we lived.

In terms of daily life, we were just people like everyone else. My brother and sister and I used to fight all the time. For instance, one of my chores was to wash the dishes. Almost every night, my brother, Boyer, would claim that he had a stomachache so he wouldn't have to wipe the dishes and put them away! I forget what Dianne's remedy was for not doing anything. But as soon as I finished those dishes, those doggone kids would come to Mom and say, "I feel better now. Can I go outside and play?" Children are con artists!

I guess we were poor but we didn't suffer any. We had a big old cookstove in the kitchen which we kept burning with wood from the firebox, and put coal in it to make the fire stay longer. Every night after supper, we put bricks in the oven. I know this sounds funny today, but each one of us had our own brick. And what we'd do is we'd take that brick when it was hot and wrap it up in newspaper so we didn't get burned. Then we'd take it upstairs and put it in that nice cold bed. Then we'd jump in the bed! And where your feet were, it was warm. As for the rest of you, you had to heat up the bed with your body.

Let me tell you, somewhere during the night, that old brick cools off. And you start to wake up, and you're thinking, Uh-oh, my feet are getting cold. And you get yourself all doubled up so that your feet are covered by your nightgown, and you go on back to sleep because there's not a thing you can do about it.

Sometimes Dianne and Boyer had to go on upstairs to bed

43

ahead of me and I got a chance to sit down there by the stove all by myself. I would sit in a rocking chair with a throw on the back to keep my shoulders warm, and I'd open the door of the oven and all that nice heat was coming out. The fire had died down enough so that I could stick my feet right in the oven. While I'd be sitting there, I'd read a mystery book from the library. Oh, it was a little bit of heaven, let me tell you! I don't think you could ask for more.

I'd read as long as I could and hope my mother didn't notice it was getting late. After a while, though, no matter how quiet I was, she'd say, "Now, Marion, it's time for you to take your brick and go on upstairs to bed."

If you had to go to the bathroom in the middle of the night, you'd get up and use the pot and then you'd get back into bed as fast as you could, while the bed was still a little warm. We had to use a chamber pot because we had an outhouse, but we didn't use the outhouse in the middle of the night. We didn't have any lights outside, and the outhouse was about fifty feet from the house. Plumbing? I think I was married before my parents had plumbing put in.

All three of us kids were in the same room. I shared a bed with my sister. My brother had his own bed, over in one corner, and we had a double bed on our side of the room. Dianne was seven years younger than me. She used to fall out of bed all the time. She was a nuisance! I would pick her up and put her back. Mom would call to me and ask what was going on. And that's when Dianne would start screeching. So I'd tell Mom, "Dianne fell out the bed and I got up and put her back in the bed, but she waited until she heard you ask what was

Marion "Strong Medicine" Gould
(RIGHT), at about age five, with her
little brother, Boyer. The photo was
taken in Philadelphia in 1927.

*going on before she started screeching!" Oh, I'm telling you, it
was something. But you see, we were just like everyone else.
We were normal people. That is something people don't understand about Indians. We're not relics in a museum. We are living in the same world as you are.*

*My brother used to chase me around the yard when I'd be
out there puttering around. He loved to throw stones. Mom had
bought him a couple pair of bib overalls and he had so many
rocks and stones in them he had to put a belt on to keep 'em
from cutting his shoulders.*

Well, in those days children had to behave. Not like today,

45

where they run the world. Discipline was not a dirty word then. One thing Indian parents wouldn't tolerate was a child who told lies. Telling the truth is very important in our culture. It is something we strive for. Anyway, Boyer learned that lesson one day after he'd been throwing rocks at me.

He would throw a stone at me and I'd jump out of the way, and he got mad because he couldn't hit me. So Boyer went inside to tell our father that I was throwing stones at him. Obviously, this was not true.

Daddy called me in to the house. He asked for my side of the story. Then he said, "You go on outdoors and I'm going to watch from the window." He decided to observe the situation before making up his mind. Now, you see, that was part of the Indian way. You observe what is happening before jumping to any conclusions. It's like when someone new comes along, we observe them, see what they're like, and what they do.

Anyway, I went outdoors and I was playing around, minding my own business, and Boyer discovered that I was back out in the yard. Boyer kept saying, "I'm going to hurt you! I'm going to hit you!" I said, "You got to catch me first," and all this time, Boyer didn't realize Daddy was watching us from the window. All of a sudden, here comes this huge barrage of stones and stuff, right at me.

Daddy was furious, and Boyer got a whipping 'cause he lied. We had a stand of sassafras trees in the yard, and he told Boyer to go get a switch from one of the trees. Boyer had this way of picking out the smallest stick, which only made Daddy even madder! Poor Boyer. He really got his tail tore up that day.

Another thing that Boyer used to do was tear up my doll

baby. He would poke out her eyes or pull out her hair. Oh, it made me so mad! Every year, a few weeks before Christmas Day, my mom would tell me that it was time for her to take my doll to a place she called "the doll hospital." On Christmas morning I would open a box with my name on it, and there was my doll, all fixed up again. And Mom had always sewed a brand-new outfit for her. I don't know where my Mom found that doll, because she wasn't white-white, like most dolls. She didn't have blue eyes, either. Her eyes were brown, like mine.

All the Indian women were good seamstresses, and my mom was one of the best. It was how she made a living. She taught me to sew when I was a tiny little girl. She gave me little scraps of material and showed me how to make clothes for my dolly. For Christmas in 1929, she got me a cast-iron toy sewing machine that actually worked. It was made by the Singer company. I still have it, and it still works. I bet today they'd call it an antique—just like me! Ha!

Christmas was the best holiday. The white people celebrated Thanksgiving, and we did, too, but our hearts were not in it. We cooked a turkey and all that, just because everyone did, but I always had the sense, when I was coming up, that Thanksgiving was not our holiday. It was for white people, a holiday that made them feel good. We don't broadcast that, it's more one of those quiet things.

Everybody in America knows the story of Thanksgiving. The Indians, up in New England, came to the rescue of the white people and they had the first Thanksgiving dinner. Okay, that's fine. But you know what? It didn't last. It wasn't long

47

before Indians from that same tribe got massacred. And this is what white people have done, time and again.

We couldn't celebrate our Indian holidays when I was coming up. We didn't dare. In those days we just wanted to survive, not get picked on because we were Indian, or have our home taken away. So we just tried to be like everyone else. We did things quietly—someone taught me to do Indian beadwork, for example—but mostly we did not want to be noticed.

I'm not saying that I had an unhappy childhood, though. I came up hard, but it was a good life.

5

When I was three years old, in 1925, my father tried to get a job with the U.S. Post Office, but they wouldn't hire him around here. He took the test and he passed, but he didn't get the job. He was "the wrong shade of white."

That's an expression that means his skin was too dark. It wasn't illegal to discriminate against people in those days.

Well, Daddy heard that the Post Office might hire him in Philadelphia, and sure enough, they did. But this meant we had to move all the way up there. That was more than an hour by train or bus, and across the Delaware River. In a way, it was still "home," though, since Philadelphia was once a part of Lenape territory. At least we were still living in the land of our ancestors.

But it was confusing, coming from the countryside, where we lived on a dirt road and had no indoor plumbing, and suddenly be thrust in this place where life—and the people—were so different.

Daddy went first and found us a place to live, then he sent for Mom and me to come join him. We lived in a little apartment, a walk-up. There was a firehouse across the street. I had a pair of roller skates, the kind that came with a key, and I tore all around our block on those skates. I was used to playing on a dirt road, not a sidewalk, and when I fell down I was surprised at how much I kept hurting my knees all the time.

We used to go window-shopping. Couldn't afford to buy anything, so we'd just stare at the mannequins in the window! We didn't have fancy stores like that where we came from. And the people—the white people!—my goodness, some of them were so rich. Secretly, I used to dream I was one of those fancy ladies. I wanted to wear a beautiful hat, and step out of a big touring car and sashay down the street.

Well, that wasn't our life, that was somebody else's! Our lives were a bit less glamorous, you might say. I remember that we walked a lot, all over the city. We went to Fairmount Park often—Mom had to be near the trees and grass, being Indian and all.

On the weekend, my mom liked to go to the Jewish and Italian markets. They had a lot of food from all over the world, and I'm sure my mother, a little Indian gal, had never seen the likes of it. The funny thing was that people had no idea she was Indian. When she went to the Jewish market, they'd speak their language to her and when she went to the Italian market, they'd speak Italian to her. They just assumed she was one of them.

Mom was lighter than Daddy, and I remember that strangers sometimes made remarks about it. There were two other couples—friends of my parents—who looked the same way. Sometimes all three families would go somewhere together on the trolley, and people would say rude things to us, like "Look at that!"

But Daddy liked Philadelphia, and he was happy with his job, though believe me, he worked hard. He had to carry these huge sacks of mail over his shoulder. Some people had wrought-iron gates they kept locked, and Daddy had to climb over the gates in order to deliver their mail. He was afraid of mean dogs and so he carried a gun. Still, he didn't complain. It was steady work and I guess he was treated pretty well.

My brother, Boyer, and my sister, Dianne, were born while we lived in Philadelphia. I guess we lived there about three years—from 1925 to 1929 or so. But after Dianne was born, Mom wanted to go home. She'd never been more than a stone's throw away from home, and I think she missed the Indian ways. Mom wasn't happy where she couldn't be outdoors. She needed to hear the sound of birds singing. She didn't think it was natural to live in a city with all the noise and dirty air and all that.

So we all moved back to the outskirts of Bridgeton, except for Daddy, who stayed in Philadelphia. He came home every weekend. This went on for years, until he retired.

Daddy's arrival on Friday nights was the best thing that happened all week. Mom always made a pot of bean soup and homemade rolls. She used to make 'em in a cupcake pan and cook 'em until there was a good crust on top, just the way he liked 'em.

A few years later, Daddy got this idea into his head that I should come back to Philadelphia and go to school there, because supposedly it was better. I went briefly to a junior high and then to Girls High School for a year.

I wasn't all that happy to be back in Philadelphia. Daddy

and I got along fine, but school was hard because they put me in three grade levels—ninth, tenth, and eleventh—all at the same time. And I wasn't ready for the upper grades like that. I was just out of sync with everyone else. For example, I'd had French, not Latin. I only lasted one year, but in terms of life experience, it was an important year for me.

I tell you what, people are people, whether they're city folks or country folks. There was plenty of prejudice. Some of the other kids would say things like, "You don't want to go around with people with knotty—kinky—hair." Well, I wasn't brought up that way. I made friends with who I wanted to be friends with. It's too bad that people can't be people without looking at color or the way you talk or something like that.

Black people didn't know I was Indian. They just assumed I was a light-skinned black girl. But for some of the really light-skinned blacks, I was too dark!

For example, there was this one girl I called "Miss Neat." She was a very light-skinned black girl, with her hair straightened just so. And she wore expensive skintight clothes and whatnot. This one day we happened to meet in the doorway and I spoke to her. I was brought up that if somebody looks at you, you smile and you speak to them and then you go about your business. But she looked at me and said, "Don't speak to me. You're not good enough to speak to me."

I had this urge to slug her but I didn't. She was lucky, 'cause Daddy had been teaching me how to box, and I'd have knocked her out cold. Daddy was worried that something would happen to me in the big city, while he was at work, and he wanted me to be able to protect myself, so he showed me a whole lot of boxing moves. Where to put my thumb. How to throw a punch. Uppercut. Right cross. Where to put my knee—ha, that's not a boxing move, but you know it will do the job if some guy is really bugging you.

My father taught me to walk differently, too. Most of the time people take small steps, but Daddy taught me how to walk military-style, with a long stride from the hip. I don't know why he wanted me to walk that way, maybe he thought it made me look like somebody you don't want to be messing with.

There was a bar I had to walk past on my way home from school, and I didn't like going past it. What I would do is cross the street a block before I got to it, walk a little ways, then cross back after I'd gone past it. Well, one day these men started yelling at me outside the bar. They started calling me "Peola" and all kinds of other things. I didn't know what it meant. That night I asked my dad about it.

It turns out there was a popular movie called Imitation of Life that had come out a year or two earlier. I think Claudette Colbert was in it. Anyway, it was about a white woman and her maid, who was black. The black lady had a daughter who could have passed. She passed, and turned her back on her mother. The daughter's name was Peola.

I guess those men outside the bar thought I was a light-skinned black person. It probably never occurred to them that I was Indian. Whatever it was they were thinking, they were making fun of me. You could hear it in the way they said it to me.

So I told Daddy about it that night, and afterward he went

out for a while. He didn't say a thing. But the next day, when I passed the bar on the other side of the street, a whole group of men rushed outside. I was surprised when they called out to me, very nicely, "How are you today, Miss Purnell?" So I guess Daddy did straighten them out. After that, they were always polite.

As far as prejudice goes, there's an enormous amount of it still out there. And I think we are going through a time when it's getting worse again. The people who are in Washington, in the Congress, they're beginning to change back and get mean. They're pretty nasty, even on television—even in public.

In order to get along with people, you have to almost talk their language, you have to try to understand them. That's what our leaders should be doing. They should be setting an example. Aren't we all supposed to be equal?

PART III

The Boy on the Bicycle

TWO AND A HALF miles from downtown Bridgeton, just beyond a forest where wild turkeys roost at night, there is a small, wood-framed bungalow that sits fifty feet back from the road, its front yard accented by a birch tree in the center and, off to the side, a newly planted maple. An impatiens plant with brilliant orange flowers beckons from a porch big enough for a single chair and a small table. With its brown-stained cedar planks and white trim, the building bears some resemblance to a gingerbread house, the kind that children decorate and eat at Christmas.

This is where Marion Strong Medicine lives, in a home her husband built himself, originally for his father.

In warmer months, the front door is usually ajar. The doorbell doesn't work—she's been meaning to fix it herself, but hasn't gotten around to it—so visitors generally announce themselves by hollering through the screen door. She is often in the kitchen, located in the back of the house.

Two large chairs face each other in the living room. A stack of newspapers and a book, *Ben Franklin's Almanac of Wit, Wisdom, and Practical Advice, by the Editors of the Old Farmer's Almanac*, sit on a coffee table.

Next door, a few hundred feet away, is her son Billy's house. On the opposite side are people to whom she is vaguely related. She refers to them as "shirttail kin," which, she says, means they are distant relatives although she doesn't know the origin of the expression. In an informal arrangement, everyone takes turns mowing the lawn, even Marion Strong Medicine, who does a small piece at a time, often by her front step if no one else has gotten around to it. There are no fences.

In the winter, another distant relative—she is not even sure who it is—stops by and plows out her gravel drive after every snowstorm. And if the boy next door doesn't get around to shoveling a path to her door, one of her great-grandsons will come over and take care of it.

She has lived on this same stretch of road since 1929. When her mother and father moved back to the Bridgeton area from Philadelphia, they bought a small, wood-frame house exactly one mile from the bungalow where she lives today.

Because her ancestors were not relocated to a reservation in the West, Marion Strong Medicine lived a fairly normal, working-class, American life, a point that she is eager to make. Like everyone else, they endured the stock market crash of 1929 and the Great Depression that followed.

The members of her tribe, however, may have fared better than most Americans during the Depression. They had survival skills—harvesting wild plants for food, hunting, and fishing—that would come in handy.

Perhaps more importantly, members of the tribe have a

deeply ingrained belief that they must look out for one another. They are conscious of the fact that they are part of a community. Although the 1920s and 1930s were an era when members of the tribe still found it necessary to hide their identity, the girl who would one day be given the name Strong Medicine knew that she was part of a clan, an extended family with roots reaching back thousands of years.

6

We did better than most people during the Depression. We already knew how to eat weeds and things like that—we just ate more of it.

We were lucky, too, because Daddy never lost his job at the U.S. Post Office in Philadelphia. They kept the mail going no matter what. And my mom still had some work as a seamstress, though not as much. She was doing lots of repairs to clothing, because people couldn't afford to buy new.

I was seven years old when the stock market crashed and you could feel the fear in the air. The economy fell apart. But you know what? I was busy being a kid. I knew times were bad but I felt pretty secure.

I loved to climb trees. I was stronger and more agile than a lot of the boys. They couldn't keep up with me. But my dream was to be a ballerina, like Maria Tallchief, the Indian ballet dancer. Unfortunately for me, I was too clumsy! So that was one dream I had to give up.

Then, when I was about fourteen, I got it in my head that I should become a detective. I wanted to be one of these glamorous women they had in the movies in the 1930s, with the high-heeled boots, the slouch hat, and the raincoat with the cape across the back.

Oh, I had an imagination! After we moved back to Bridgeton, in the summertime I would take a blanket and I'd throw it on the ground and I'd lay out there with a couple of throw pillows and watch those fluffy clouds, just watch how they moved. I was reading some stories from England from long ago, and the first thing you'd know, in the clouds, I could see the shape of a castle, and maybe the drawbridge.

I went to the library a lot. That was one of the places I was allowed to go. I'd pick out books and bring them home. I loved mysteries. I could just lose myself in books. Just lose myself.

If we had been living on a reservation out west somewhere, I wouldn't have had a normal life. I doubt I would have had a good library to go to, like the one we had in Bridgeton. And I don't think I would have had a good public school education, along with all the other kids—white, black, and Indian. Although some schools in South Jersey were segregated, Bridgeton schools were not. And New Jersey schools have always been very good.

As long as I did my homework and my chores at home, I could go ahead and read what I wanted. And if I got tired of doing that, I'd go and get my embroidery out. I had to be doing something all the time.

I also did Indian beadwork from a very early age. I don't even remember being taught how to do it. I just remember Mom handing me a blouse with a design on it, and I would start beading.

Of course, we didn't have television. That wasn't even

invented yet. We listened to the radio, but reception wasn't too good in our neck of the woods. If we had a little bit of money, we might go to the movies. There were three movie theaters in Bridgeton back when I was coming up. One was for people of color. One was for white people but it had a balcony for people of color. And the other one, I believe, was not segregated at all.

Believe it or not, the one with the balcony was also segregated by time of day. In other words, colored people could sit downstairs in roped-off sections at certain showings. It was nuts, but that's the way it was. Of course, being Indian, I was expected to sit with the black folks. I really didn't think anything of it. When you're a kid, you think that what you see around you is normal. You don't necessarily question it.

In the summertime, when there was an electric storm at night, that was our "show." We would sit at the dining room table—a safe distance from the window—and Mom would turn off the lights and pull back the curtain and we would sit there and watch the Creator do his thing.

Mostly, we read a lot in those days. My favorite magazine was National Geographic. I remember the first time Daddy brought home an issue, in 1929. I'm telling you, if you want to know about the world, that's the thing to read.

Daddy wanted us to improve ourselves. He made sure I knew ten new words every week, not just how to spell 'em but how they were used. Oh, golly, that was horrendous. Some of them seemed like they were a foot long. He would come up with a sentence and say, "I want you to tell me what it means." He was always testing me, pushing me with my schoolwork.

I got to the point—I think I was in eleventh grade—where I was ahead of the other kids because of the work my father made me do. My English teacher was making everybody come up and read essays we had written. She got to mine and she told me, "Marion, come up here for a minute." I didn't know what was going on. And she said, "Marion, did you write this?" I said, "Yes, I wrote this. You can see it's my handwriting." But she said, "You've got some big words here, and I don't think you know them."

I told her to try me. So, she did. She was very surprised. But she did believe me, after testing me.

Now I am grateful to my father that he pushed me in school. I know he was doing what was best for me. I have a high school degree, which is more than a lot of Indian people were able to accomplish. In my generation, especially because of the Depression, it was pretty common for Indian children to drop out of school to help at home. A lot of Indians my age can't read or write, and some of them are embarrassed about it. I don't think they should feel that way, though. Some of them have more common sense and more knowledge than people with advanced college degrees to their name.

Indian children were expected to help their parents. Nothing was more important than the family, than getting food on the table. The boys helped in the fields and with the farm animals, if there were any. The girls, well, we had to do chores in the house.

Personally, I would rather have been outdoors doing the boys' job! The worst was laundry day. Oh, how I hated that. All I can say is, Thank goodness for the person who invented the modern washing machine. We used to have to pump the water, put a big tub on the stove to heat it, and then carry it out back to the shed. It weighed a ton, I'm telling you. Mom and I had to lift it together. We had a glass washboard and you would put the material against the washboard and scrub the daylights out of it. You had to fill the tub with water three times—the water you washed in, the first rinse, and a second rinse.

When I was coming up you didn't ask a whole lot of questions. You just did as you were told. If my mom says, "Come on, we got to go out and work in the garden," that's what I did. I didn't give her any grief about it. If it was summertime and I wasn't going to school, Mom would get me up in the morning and I would go out and help hoe or something like that. Vegetables had to be picked, vegetables had to be cleaned and canned. That was part of life.

My mom depended on me a lot. She was working full time as a dressmaker, so she was always busy. Mom never learned to drive, so she would walk to people's houses or maybe take the bus that went into town. Some of her customers came by the house.

There was one family that seemed to need her all the time. Their name was Ritter, and they owned one of the two big catsup factories in town. They were well off. They were white. Well, that goes without saying. Anybody who was well off was white.

Mom went over to their house rather than Mrs. Ritter coming over to ours. Mrs. Ritter had everything all set up. She always needed her clothes adjusted, for some reason. And Mr.

Ritter, he was just as bad. He'd have a whole pile of shirts where the collar, or the cuffs, were beginning to fray a little bit, so Mom would turn the material around so they'd get twice the wear. We used to laugh because Mr. Ritter and his wife didn't even know how to fix the drawstring in his pajamas. They didn't seem to be able to do anything without Mom.

They were decent folks, though, and as far as I know they were not prejudiced toward us being Indian. They even recommended Mom to some friends of theirs in New York, people who were in the imported olive oil business. Mom used to go up there and do their sewing, after I was old enough to be left in charge of Boyer and Dianne. These people would see to it that she got to and from New York. I don't think Mom minded going. Maybe she was glad to get rid of us kids! At any rate, it was probably the furthest she ever went in her life, and I think she had a good time.

It's hard to believe it now, but for thousands of years, New York was part of our territory. We were the tribe that "sold" Manhattan to the Dutch for twenty-four dollars, and people have been laughing at us ever since. It's in the textbooks and it makes us look like a bunch of fools. Well, we weren't fools. We just didn't understand the white man's idea of buying and selling land. No one is sure what happened, but probably my people thought they were accepting that twenty-four dollars as a gift for permitting the white man to hunt on the land. Nothing more.

At any rate, Mom used to go to Manhattan during the thirties to do work for these white people. And she had regular customers like the Ritters, so that helped pay the bills.

The Boy on the Bicycle

The Ritters and another family, the Pritchards, owned the two competing companies that made tomato catsup in Bridgeton, but I couldn't tell you what's happened to those businesses now. They are long gone. I suppose they got bought up by some huge conglomerate. But I remember a time, in late summer and fall, when the whole town of Bridgeton smelled like tomato catsup. We didn't mind! People used to think it was grand because it meant jobs. The farmers would come in from the countryside with their horse-drawn wagons loaded sky-high with the most beautiful tomatoes you ever saw. The wagons would be lined up near the old high school, up on the hill, all the way through downtown and around the corner.

Even though Mom worked full time as a seamstress, she had a magnificent garden. You would be hard-pressed to find Indian people without a garden, and some people—like Mr. Cuff, he's ninety-three years old—still plant it the Indian way, in alternating rows of corn, beans, and squash. That is the classic staple of the Indian diet. And me—I still have my flowers and my herb garden.

When I was coming up, we never bought hardly anything in a jar because we canned everything ourselves. Every kind of fruit imaginable. That was life! But then we were always glad later. When summer was over and we were back in school, Mom would surprise us by making an upside-down cake, with a thick layer of blackberries on the bottom. You would have it with milk or whipped cream; it all depended how much money you had in the house.

Now, my mom was a great cook, and we didn't miss anything. She would make macaroni and cheese with eggs in it. On

Sunday mornings, she would make a stack of blueberry pancakes a foot and a half tall, and my brother and I would see which one could eat the most. You'd pour molasses all over them and, my Lord, did that ever stick to your ribs. And sometimes we would have salt mackerel and eggs and fried potatoes with our pancakes. You wouldn't be hungry again all day long.

On school days, we usually ate hot oatmeal or Postum or maybe Cream of Wheat 'cause Mom was in a hurry to get us out the door and get to work on her sewing. We had to walk to school, even in the snow. I would walk all the way to the high school from my house. It was about two miles, but I used to do it in a half hour if the weather was good.

There weren't any sidewalks that far out, so you had to walk in the road, and when it snowed, you hoped a car might go by and make a path for you. It used to snow much more often than it does now. Sometimes Mom kept the younger kids at home because the snowdrifts were so high but I got sent to school, no matter what.

There were kids who came from farms that were way out in the countryside and they had to walk, too, or if they were really lucky they might hitch a ride, though there weren't many cars on the road. There weren't many school buses. I remember one boy, he walked about six miles each way, and one morning he showed up at school with frostbite on his face, hands, and feet. But that was part of country living.

The roads to school were probably once Indian paths, and I used to wonder, when I'd walk along, what it would have been like to be a Lenape maiden in the old days, before the white people came. I imagine it was quite pleasant. I used to think,

The Boy on the Bicycle

"If I had been born at a different time, I wouldn't have to go to school! Maybe I would be doing something more sensible, like sitting by a fire and doing beadwork. Oh, and I would have my pick of warriors to choose from!"

Well, as it turned out, I did have my pick of warriors. There was one fellow who would sit under my window at night in the summertime and sing and play the guitar. It really annoyed me, though, because he smoked, and the fumes would go up in the air and into my window! So one time I leaned out the window and I called down to him, "Hey, don't you know that smoking's not good for you?" and I slammed the window shut. Well, that was the end of that. I ran him off.

Another fellow—he was too old for me—used to wait 'til I walked past his house on my way home from school and try to walk me home. That one lifted weights and would strut around like a peacock on his front porch when I walked by. Oh, he was ridiculous. I used to call him "Muscle Man" behind his back.

But the truth is, I only had eyes for one. His name was Wilbur Gould, and although he didn't know it for quite a long while, I had already picked him out.

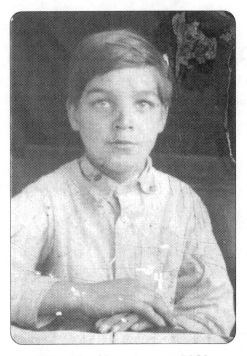

Wilbur Gould at age ten in 1929.

7

One day when I was in the eighth grade, I was out front of my parents' house and I looked up from the book I was reading, and I saw a bicycle with two kids on it coming down the road. A boy was sitting on the seat with his feet sticking out, trying to balance himself. A little girl—his little sister, it turned out—was standing up, pedaling as hard as she could.

That was the first time I spied Wilbur Gould.

I have no idea why, but from that moment on, I started keeping an eye out for him. I couldn't help it. He had an aunt who lived down the road from me, and that's where he and his sister, Margaret, were headed that day.

I didn't get to talk to him for a while, though. Finally, later that summer, my cousins and I were sitting out on the front lawn, near the driveway. He came on down the road—this time, without his little sister—and he got off his bike and sat down on the ground with the rest of us. He didn't say much of anything. I, of course, was thrilled just to get a good, up-close look at him, but I tried to act like I didn't notice him.

But then a weird thing happened. There was a girl who lived across the street, and she saw him sitting with us. Well, here she came. She walked straight up to him and smacked him alongside the head! And knocked him over! She said, "I'll teach you! You told me you weren't going to come around here. Don't you speak to me!" Then she marched back across the street.

My cousins almost died laughing. I was thinking, "Lord have mercy, what have we got here?" But I tried not to laugh. I never did find out what that was all about. It was just one of those stupid things—we were all maybe fourteen years old. Maybe she liked him. Maybe he said something to her. Who knows? It didn't deter me.

Once school started again, I went out of my way to look for him. He was in the grade ahead of me, so we weren't in any classes together. When I got to school in the morning, I used to run up the stairs to a landing where there was a window. And I would wait there and watch out the window for Wilbur and his brother to walk up the hill to school.

Meantime, there was another boy who really liked me. It seemed like I was always running away from that guy. I would go up to the second floor from a different staircase, go down the hall, then duck through the auditorium so that I would miss him. I don't know how, but he always managed to find me. Once, when I was dodging him, I ran right smack into him. And the English teacher—she was always watching things—she told him, "Marion doesn't want to talk to you. She's not waiting for you to come. Go on, get out of here." She had figured out that I was interested in Wilbur. I guess it was pretty obvious—to everyone, evidently, except Wilbur. Looking back, I think it may have been the worst-kept secret in town.

Wilbur took a long time to come around. He was sort of

"hard to get." He didn't have a lot of girlfriends. He stayed to himself, except for his little brother. They got into trouble together a lot. You'd hear their names being called to report to the principal's office.

Now, that other guy, he was okay. But he didn't appeal to me as the person for the rest of my life. Oh, boy, did he like me, though. I had one heck of a time. I think today they call it stalking.

I ended up going to the prom with him, though, because Wilbur didn't ask me. By then, Wilbur had finally figured out that I liked him and we started seeing each other a little bit. But the problem was that Wilbur didn't dance. Well, he danced, but he was not very good, and he didn't seem interested in improving himself, so he wouldn't go to dances. And dancing was a big, big thing in those days.

Eventually, I kind of nudged him to a compromise. I said, "Hey, I don't care that you don't like to dance. Let's go out anyway." So we did. And what happened was, we would go to a church dance or whatever, and I would dance with different men who asked me. Meanwhile, Wilbur danced with the old ladies who didn't have a partner. He always said he did that because it was a nice thing to do. Frankly, the old ladies didn't mind him stepping all over his feet. They were just thrilled to be out on the dance floor.

This worked fine for everybody. And Wilbur never seemed to get jealous of the other men who danced with me. Of course, I would rather have been dancing with Wilbur. But what can you do? You can't reject a person over something like that.

Wilbur was almost three years older than me, but one year

ahead of me in school, on account of my having been in high school in Philadelphia for a year. He graduated in 1939, and I graduated in 1940.

It's funny, I don't remember ever talking to him about marriage. One day he just showed up with a ring, and that was that. We didn't have a wedding the way a lot of folks do. We didn't have any money! It wasn't a big fuss. I put on my best dress (no, it wasn't white; it was blue with a pattern of small flowers) and I met Wilbur at the preacher's house. We got married in the preacher's parlor. We had two witnesses: our friends Bill and Marion, who were already married, stood up for us. This was July 11, 1940. Sometimes that seems like a long time ago, and sometimes it doesn't.

Wilbur began building us a house, one mile down the road from my parents. He started on it even before we got married. It was a "work in progress," you might say. It wasn't finished but we could live in it. We didn't care that it wasn't perfect. We were just glad to have a roof over our heads and to be together.

He worked on the house when he had time. During the day, he worked at the Philadelphia Navy Yard. He and a couple of other guys drove to the ferry landing and took the boat across the Delaware River. It was good pay and Wilbur enjoyed the work.

I look back on those days and I don't say, "Oh, I sure am sorry that I didn't have a bigger house. Or a set of English china." No, I look back and say, "We loved each other, we were healthy, we were broke most of the time but we were happy living the simple life."

Before long I was expecting our first baby. I didn't know a great deal about what to expect in terms of giving birth, so I

Wilbur Gould building their home, 1941.

*studied a book my mom had at home. It was a health book that
had a chapter on pregnancy and childbirth. To tell you the
truth, I really was not too concerned. I knew my mom and my
aunt would be there, and the same woman doctor who delivered
me, so I didn't worry.*

*We didn't talk about sex that much in those days, and you
sure didn't strut around with your body parts hanging out like
the girls do now. And when you were pregnant, you were dis-
creet about it. Modesty is something that has just completely
gone out the window.*

*Now people even invite their older children to be present
when the baby is born! And all kinds of relatives, even
neighbors! And they photograph the whole thing. I don't get
that at all.*

These new generations are something else. Frankly, I think some things should be private. That is part of the Indian way—there are some things that are better kept between a man and his wife, or a mother and daughter. Within the family.

When my time came, Wilbur called the doctor, who came directly to the house. Wilbur went out in the field behind our house during all the excitement. I think he was cutting cornstalks down. There I am lying in the bed, bringing Billy into the world, and my husband is as far away as he could get. That's the way it was in those days. Frankly, that was fine with me. I had my mom, my aunt Mary, the woman doctor, and her nurse. I had four experienced women there. I figured if they can't help me, nobody can! What good's a man in a situation like that?

I think I might have passed out because I really don't remember much. But everything worked out fine. Billy was a beautiful, healthy baby. He weighed eight pounds.

Nowadays you hear about women having babies at forty-five, even older. What are they thinking? A lot of them have to be operated on, because their bodies don't "give" anymore. I think it's better to have your children early and get 'em out of the way.

A year and a half after Billy was born, our son Mark was born. He weighed just under eight pounds. He was born at home, too. So by the time I was twenty years old, I had two little baby boys to look after. I enjoyed it. I was a natural mother. It never occurred to me whether or not to have children, it was just something you did. Especially if you were Indian, it was just something that was really valued.

The Boy on the Bicycle

When I was expecting Mark, I tried not to let Billy get jealous. Billy was curious and he noticed that Mommy was beginning to grow a belly. So I said, "Billy, I'm going to tell you a story. But you're going to have to wait a couple of months so I can show you what the story's all about." So I gave him something else to do and he forgot all about it. But Mommy came through. By the time he brought it up again, the baby was moving. So I put his hand on my tummy so that he could feel it moving around. And I showed him pictures of himself when he was a newborn baby. I said, "This is what you looked like when you were a tiny baby inside Mommy. But you're going to have to wait, 'cause the baby won't come for another couple of months. You're going to have to help Mommy around the house and help Mommy pick up things. You can't throw things on the floor anymore and Mommy will pick them up. You're going to have to pick them up yourself." See, that way I helped him and helped myself a little bit at the same time.

The way I see it, there's a right way and a wrong way to do just about everything. I didn't want to overload Billy with all kinds of details about childbirth that he wasn't ready to hear.

I learned all this stuff from my mother and her sisters—just from observing the way they did things. Indians don't "leave" our original families that we were born into. When we get married, we're just adding on. This business about a woman leaving her parents' house, well, I can't speak for other tribes but I never saw that in Lenape culture. A man wouldn't dare move his wife too far from her mother and father. In fact, it was more the opposite. The man became part of the woman's family.

If I got mad at Wilbur, I would go back to my parents'

house. *The boys had a little red wagon, and I would set them in it, along with a little bag for our clothes. And I'd pull them in the wagon down the road to my parents' house and stay there until I'd cooled down. If I was really mad, I'd stay there until Wilbur walked over there and said he was sorry and asked me to come back.*

The funny thing is, I can't remember a single reason why we quarreled. When you're young, you get upset about the dumbest things. That's one of the interesting things about growing old. Now I look back and I say to myself, "What was I thinking?"

PART IV

"I Am Sorry to Inform You . . ."

MARION STRONG MEDICINE is peering out the car window, trying to remember exactly where, along a narrow street in downtown Bridgeton, the buses had lined up to take the young men away, ultimately to North Africa, Europe, the Pacific, and other parts of the world too far away to imagine.

Sixty-three years have passed since she kissed Wilbur good-bye here, among the throng of wives, mothers, sisters, elderly fathers, and wistful little brothers who bid farewell, in some cases forever, to the able-bodied men of Cumberland County. Farmers, college boys, factory workers, and fishermen alike were leaving home to fight in the Second World War.

The Lenape Indians, typical among Native Americans, were ready and willing to do their part. American Indians, generally speaking, are a patriotic people. In fact, during World War II, one third of the eligible Indian population served in the military, or three times the rate (about 13 percent) of the general population. Some tribes even declared war on Germany, among them the Chippewa, Sioux, and Iroquois.

More than sixteen million Americans served in World War II. Of that number, only about 4 percent were women. Left in charge of the "home front," American women carried out an important role. They raised the children, ran family farms, and worked in jobs held previously by men, which kept the economy going. About three million women worked in war plants. Still others, such as Marion Strong Medicine, took nonmilitary assembly line jobs that had previously been filled mostly by men.

During the war, Cumberland County, New Jersey, was no longer the sleepy outpost it had been for hundreds of years. Soon the skies would be filled with small fighter planes—Republic P-47 "Thunderbolts"—as some fifteen hundred pilots received advanced combat training at a converted airport in Millville, a dozen miles from Bridgeton. It was commonplace to see Thunderbolts flying through the sky, spinning and diving—and occasionally crashing. One midair collision claimed the life of two young pilots. In all, fourteen young men from the Millville Army Air Field lost their lives, their planes crashing into farmland or the Atlantic Ocean.

The reality of the war could also be seen in the town of Seabrook, about six miles north of Bridgeton. Facing a shortage of crop workers, Charles F. Seabrook and his three sons, owners of a twenty-thousand-acre farm, persuaded the federal government to let them recruit 2,500 Japanese Americans who otherwise would have been incarcerated in internment camps in the West.

"I Am Sorry to Inform You . . ."

Cumberland County was changing. The war's impact was felt most keenly, however, by the absence of Cumberland County's young men. Some never came back, and for those who did, their lives were forever changed.

Reported Missing

PFC Wilbur Gould, Jr., who has been attached to the Third Army, under General Patton, was recently reported missing in action. He is married and has two small sons. His father, Wilbur Gould, Sr., resides at R. D. 4.

Newspaper photo and caption from December 1944 (*The Bridgeton News*) announcing that Wilbur Gould was missing in action during what came to be called the Battle of the Bulge.

8

Wilbur got his draft notice in 1942, the year after Pearl Harbor was attacked and the U.S. got into the war. Wilbur was ready to go—he would have enlisted if it hadn't been for me and the boys.

In those days, the army was still segregated—there was the Negro army and there was the regular army, which was for white men. Wilbur told them he was Indian, but the officer in charge didn't think he was dark enough to be in the Negro army. As I said before, Wilbur had blue eyes because he had a little Irish blood, and I guess the army officer couldn't make sense of that. He insisted that Wilbur be put in with the whites.

When Wilbur's little brother, Jesse, enlisted, I think they were going to put him in the Negro army, because he was quite a bit darker, with dark brown eyes. But Jesse pointed out that his own brother was in the white army already, so they put him in there, too. But when my brother, Boyer, enlisted, I think he was put in the Negro army.

Once he was in the army, though, Wilbur said he was never discriminated against on account of being Indian. He told his army pals he was Indian, and no one had any problem with it

Mark (LEFT), the future Chief, and older
brother, Billy, circa 1945.

*at all. He was just one of the guys. I have a picture of him that
he sent, goofing around with his army buddies. One of his
friends is wearing a top hat, of all things, and sitting on
Wilbur's shoulders.*

*When it was time for Wilbur to leave home, we boarded up
our house—it wasn't completely finished anyway—and I
moved back to my parents' house with the boys. On the morning he left, we went into downtown Bridgeton to see him off.
Not just me and the boys, but his dad and sisters were there,
too. A lot of men from the area were all leaving at the same
time. They had a staging area for the buses. Wilbur found his
bus, he kissed me good-bye, and suddenly he was gone. It was
an empty feeling, let me tell you.*

They took him to Florida for basic training. They decided to make him a forward scout, which meant that his job would be to go ahead of the troops and check things out, like what the enemy was doing, how many there were, and so on. It was an especially dangerous job. After training, he was sent overseas, to Europe.

I thought that when he left for training, I wouldn't get to see him again, but I had a nice surprise. After training, the army let him come home for two days before they sent him to Europe.

Those two days are a blur. This time, Wilbur didn't want me to come see him off. He thought saying good-bye again would be horrible, so he went to the station alone. He took the train to New York, where he rejoined his unit, and they sailed to Europe on one of those enormous troopships.

Billy (LEFT) and Mark, at ages five and four, circa 1946.

I was twenty-one years old when he went overseas, with two little boys to look after. The army didn't pay the men much, so even though Wilbur sent me his army pay, I had to find a way to make a little money so we could eat. I worked extra hard on my garden and Pop, Wilbur's father, would take my vegetables to sell at the farmers' market. I didn't want any kind of work that would take me away from the boys because they were so little, and I got a job up the road a ways at the Birds Eye factory, where they were freezing vegetables. It sounds funny now, but it was state of the art at the time. This fellow named Birdseye had invented a method of freezing vegetables. It was fresher than canned.

My job was to work on an assembly line and count the number of peas that went into a certain-sized cardboard container. I almost went mad, I'm telling you. And I was so tired from being worried about Wilbur and chasing after the boys that I used to fall asleep on the assembly line! They had these tall stools that we had to sit on, and they were very uncomfortable but I managed to nod off anyway. The weirdest thing is, I got so I could do my job even though I was basically asleep. The woman in charge would say, "Marion, I declare, I think you were asleep counting those peas again today!"

My boys gave me a lot of joy, but it was a good thing I was young and could keep after them. One thing they loved to do was climb trees, even when they were tiny. You turn around, and they were up in a tree someplace. Maybe they got that from me, because any chance I got as a little girl, I was hanging upside down from a tree.

One time, I left my sister-in-law in charge of the boys while I walked downtown to do some shopping. I don't know why—some instinct, I suppose—but I turned around and glanced back at the house. And I could hardly believe my eyes. My two little boys had somehow climbed up on the roof! Lord only knows how they were doing it, because that is a steep roof. I wouldn't have wanted to climb up it myself, even when I was growing up.

Of course, your first instinct is to scream and run over there. But I stifled that urge. I figured if I startled them, they'd get scared and fall off. So I walked casually back to the house, trying not to look at them, and then I coaxed them down.

I sometimes put the boys on a leash. I'm not kidding. I had a harness and a leash for each of them when they were toddlers. That way, when I was in a store and had my hands full, I could keep 'em out of trouble. Billy wasn't so bad. If he got away from me all he would do is run and hide. But Mark—he was something else. He would be gone in a flash. He was very curious, and he would disappear in a second—not just down an aisle but behind the counter, maybe up the shelves.

Raising children is the hardest job in the world. I got a lot of help from my family and Wilbur's family, too, so it's not like I did it alone. But it was a lot harder without their father around.

I tried not to think of Wilbur every minute of the day, but he was always on my mind no matter what. For the only time in my life, I was scared. We had just started our life together and this darned war come along and had to mess everything up. Yes, it was a good cause and our country really didn't have any choice but to fight. But sometimes you just felt selfish and wished the whole mess would just go away.

In those days you couldn't get instant information like you can now. There was no Internet and all that. There was no such thing as a cell phone, so it's not like a man in the army could call from anywhere. People didn't even make long-distance calls, not often anyway, because they were very expensive.

Instead, everything went by regular mail, and censors screened everything to make sure there wasn't any secret information. There were big delays because the mail was coming and going from the war zone. Sometimes you'd get a batch of letters, all at the same time. Other times you'd get nothing at all for a long stretch, even though we wrote to each other all the time. Mostly we had to send these little letters, not a postcard but a very thin sheet of paper that fit into a thin little envelope.

Then one day I got a telegram. My sister and my mom were home, and we were all terrified. Just sick, you know.

So I opened it. It said:

I AM SORRY TO INFORM YOU THAT YOUR HUSBAND IS MISSING IN ACTION.

I didn't cry. Not inside the house, anyway. I went outside to be alone. I had no idea if I would ever see him again, but I knew the odds were against it.

All I knew was that he was missing somewhere on the Western Front. It was only later that I learned that it happened during the Battle of the Bulge, which had been a bloodbath for our side. A lot of American men were killed.

I kept looking at the last letter I got from him, which was dated December 18, 1944. Wilbur was never one for going to church, but he seemed to have found the Lord while he was overseas. He wrote: "All of the boys are very tired. Most of our comfort comes from the Bible. I have faith in the Lord that it won't be long. I think if we all ask Him it will soon be over. Please keep praying for all of us over here."

During the next few weeks, when I couldn't stand it anymore, I asked my sister or my mom to look after the boys and I went for long walks in the middle of the night, if the moon was shining. I needed to sort things out in my mind, the way I have always done, the Indian way—by breathing the fresh air and being alone with nature.

I would walk from my parents' house all the way to the house my husband and I had been building for ourselves— where we had been living when he was called by the army. Sometimes I'd look at that house and it made me feel better. Sometimes it made me feel worse. After a while, I'd walk back to my parents' again.

I was so restless.

Finally, one day I got another telegram and I thought, "This is it. He's dead."

But it said they'd found him alive! Oh, I'm telling you, it was one of the happiest days of my life. The telegram said, "Am pleased to inform you your husband Private Wilbert

Gould Jr. returned to duty 31 December. Dunlop, Acting the Adjutant General."

I didn't get this telegram until the end of January 1945. That's how long it took the army to get me the information.

I still have that telegram, and I keep it in my dresser drawer. I was going to give it to one of the boys. But I just can't let it go.

Another Bridgeton Soldier
Listed as Missing in Action

PFC Wilbur Gould, Jr., 25, is missing in action somewhere on the Western Front, while serving as an infantryman with the Third Army.

Notification was received by his wife, Marion Gould, who resides at an R. D. 4 address, with their two sons. According to the War Department telegram, PFC Gould was reported missing on December 23. He had been in the service eight months, overseas two and a half months. Before entering the service Gould was employed at the Philadelphia Navy Yard.

Mrs. Gould said that the last letter she received from her husband was dated December 18 in which he said: "All of the boys are very tired. Most of our comfort comes from the Bible. I have faith in the Lord that it won't be long. I think if we all ask Him it will soon be over. Please keep praying for all of us over here."

Gould has a younger brother, Jeffe, who is a tank driver somewhere in Belgium.

Newspaper article (*The Bridgeton News*) announcing that Wilbur Gould was missing in

Her Husband Safe

Mrs. Wilbur Gould, R. D. 4, Bridgeton, received a telegram yesterday from the War Department advising that her husband, previously reported missing in action January 6, had returned to active duty.

action during what came to be called the Battle of the Bulge. Also, newspaper notice from January 1945 that he was safe.

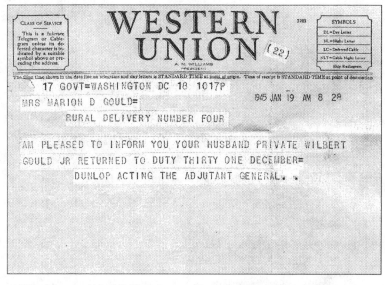

WESTERN UNION

A. N. WILLIAMS
PRESIDENT

1201 (22)

The filing time shown in the date line on telegrams and day letters is STANDARD TIME at point of origin. Time of receipt is STANDARD TIME at point of destination

17 GOVT=WASHINGTON DC 18 1017P

1945 JAN 19 AM 8 28

MRS MARION D GOULD=

    RURAL DELIVERY NUMBER FOUR

AM PLEASED TO INFORM YOU YOUR HUSBAND PRIVATE WILBERT GOULD JR RETURNED TO DUTY THIRTY ONE DECEMBER=

    DUNLOP ACTING THE ADJUTANT GENERAL.

The January 19, 1945, telegram from the War Department informing Marion "Strong Medicine" Gould that Wilbur Gould, who had been missing in action, was alive and had found his way back to his unit.

9

The war in Europe went on for another five months, ending in May 1945. Wilbur's unit got word, while they were still in Europe, that they were going to be sent to the Pacific front. But the Japanese surrendered in August. The war was over.

We were all just as pleased as punch that the men were coming home. Everyone was just worn out by the war. You just wanted to move on with your life. You wanted to live a normal life and make plans for the future, for a change.

I got word that Wilbur would be coming home, but I didn't know when. I started moving out of my parents' house and back into the house Wilbur had been building for us. I got busy! I sent a letter to Wilbur telling him that I was going to get our house ready. I had the boards taken off the windows, and I started moving things in there again.

Wilbur had two older sisters, Catherine and Isabel. One day, Catherine was helping me. The house was looking pretty good. She went outside to do something—hang laundry on the clothesline, I think. I was in the bedroom.

Suddenly I heard her screaming, and I looked out the bedroom window. She had dropped what she was doing and run toward the road like a crazy woman. I saw a man with a duffel

94

bag over his shoulder. He was walking up the road and across the yard, and next thing I know I realize it's Wilbur.

His sister just about knocked him over. It looked like she flew through the air! She wrapped her arms around him and she wouldn't let go. He was laughing, and his sister was hanging off him as he tried to keep walking toward the house.

I don't know why, but I couldn't move. I was standing there in the bedroom looking out the window. I heard the screen door open and his voice calling my name. He had untangled himself from his sister and was coming in the house to find me.

You laugh 'til you cry, that's all I can say. Once I put my arms around him, I understood why his sister had trouble letting loose of him. I didn't want to let him go, either.

Wilbur had wanted it to be a surprise, so he had taken a cab from the train station and told the cabdriver to go past the house. Then he had him stop. He got out, and he walked back to our house on that old dirt road. I think he also wanted a few moments to be alone, to walk down that familiar old road, look around, and get his bearings. I think he wanted to see things as they were, the way he remembered it, before a commotion started.

And, oh boy, a commotion is what we had, as soon as people figured out what was happening. All the people up and down the road—most of them were kinfolk, after all—heard all this screaming and hollering going on, and they came running out of their houses and rushed over. Everybody was happy for some good news. This war affected everyone— didn't matter what color you were, you were either serving overseas or you were related to somebody who was. Our little tight-knit Lenape community was just thrilled to have one of our boys home again, especially since we thought we'd lost him.

I don't think the excitement ever died down that day. People came out of the woodwork to say hello, then rushed home to get ready for the big party we would have that night. All the ladies used up their rations to make their best dishes. We had macaroni and cheese, chicken, beets—Wilbur loved beets—and a ham and I don't know what all. There was Lenape corn pudding, fruit pies. Was there a cake? Oh, my, I would guess there were fifteen to twenty cakes. The liquor was flowing, too. Anything anybody had been hoarding, we ate it or drank it up that night.

As always with Indian people, it was tiny babies and old folks, and every age in between. Wilbur's mom had died years before, but his dad was still living and was an honored guest at the party. Billy and Mark were then about four and three years old. For most of the night, Wilbur had the boys in his lap or in his arms. If the moon had fallen out of the sky that night, I wouldn't have noticed. Wilbur was home!

But I noticed, almost right away, that he didn't talk much about what had happened to him in the war. This became apparent to me, especially after his brother Jesse came home. Jesse had been a tank driver in Belgium, and he and Wilbur built him a house on the other side of their father's. We lived on one side of Pop, and Jesse and his family lived on the other. So we saw Jesse all the time. And he seemed to talk about the war a lot, like the other men.

There were only two stories that Wilbur would share. One was his backpack being blown clear off his back by a German sniper. He had taken some photos of me and the boys with him, and those pictures, and everything else in his backpack, were blown to bits. But Wilbur didn't have a scratch on him.

The other story was about a little old French lady and her cow. He says his unit came across her one day, and she was trying to milk her cow but it was so cold she couldn't hang on to the teats. Her hands were almost frozen. So he gave her a pair of gloves he had. See, that is the Indian way. You don't let your elders suffer. No way.

She thanked him and he left. But he hears a big commotion, hears her screaming, so he goes back. So this guy who he was friends with, somebody from his unit, he had gone in the barn and saw this old lady with a pair of gloves that were American, part of the American army gear. And this guy was hitting this old lady! This boy was someone Wilbur knew well, somebody he knew from going overseas on the boat with him and all. They had been friends up until this point.

So Wilbur went back there and asked this guy, "What are you doing? What's going on?" And the guy said, "This old lady stole these gloves!" So Wilbur got into a fight with this guy and he told him, "If you don't want me to kill you, you better take your hands off her. She didn't have any gloves to milk her cow, and I gave her a pair of my gloves, and you better leave her alone!" And that was that. He and the other guy didn't speak to each other after that.

There was another guy, though, that Wilbur stayed friends with for many years, until the guy died. His name was Art and he was from St. Louis, where he owned a baseball camp. About twenty years after the war, he came to visit us and brought his wife. We went to Atlantic City, had dinner and all, and walked the boardwalk. The two men didn't talk much about the war, though. The only thing I knew, from what Art said, was that he had been separated from the unit and Wilbur volunteered to go back and look for him. Art had been wounded and fell behind, but Wilbur found him and carried him back.

Twenty-five years passed before Wilbur talked about being MIA—missing in action. And then, it was only because a man who was interested in history, a man from our tribe, came and asked him. After Wilbur told the man his story, you might think that would have loosened him up, but it didn't. Wilbur still didn't talk about it, hardly at all, all the way up to the time he died.

This is what happened to him: Even before the Battle of the Bulge, things had been pretty terrible for his unit. It was pretty common that they slept outside in the open air, and it was winter and bitter cold. Wilbur said sometimes he would take off his coat, put it around a small tree, then button himself into it to stay upright and awake to keep from freezing to death. Several times he woke up in the morning and his friends were lying on the ground frozen solid and he was the only one left living. Other times, he'd wake up in the morning and find one or more of his buddies shot dead by German snipers during the night.

Then came the Battle of the Bulge. Since Wilbur was a for-ward scout, he was up front as usual. But this time, he and sev-

eral other Americans were captured by the Germans and taken
to a prisoner of war camp.

He was there a short time when a German soldier told him
that he might be able to help him escape. This German soldier
said, "I'm Frank, and I'm from Brooklyn." Wilbur never
learned what that guy's story was, but probably he had relatives in Germany, went over there and got stuck there, and was
drafted. We have no idea, really. All I know is that a guy from
Brooklyn helped my husband, a Lenape Indian, escape from a
German prison camp! Now if that don't beat all, I don't know
what does.

So this guy, Frank, tells Wilbur that the Germans were
planning to execute the prisoners when they brought food into
the prison that night. He said wait until they arrive, then go all
the way to the back of the prison and slip out where the car
came in—it would be the only chance.

My husband passed the information to the other guys, but
most of them didn't want to try it. It was bitter cold, and
escaped prisoners were shot right away. And who knew if the
information was right?

But my husband and another buddy or two—I was never
clear how many—decided to chance it. They did what the
guy, Frank, said. They slipped through the gate when it
opened, and made a run for it through the countryside. The
German soldiers figured out pretty quickly that they'd escaped
and set out after them. For the next couple of weeks, they were
on the run.

Wilbur said the French people they encountered did everything they could to protect them. These were all very poor peo-

ple, country people. At one point, a farmer and his family buried Wilbur and his pals in this great big pile of manure. Wilbur said the farmer told them, "Hurry, hurry, hurry, hurry, hurry." The Germans were right on their trail, and sure enough when they saw the manure pile, they were suspicious. They took these pitchforks with these great big old tines on 'em and they poked and poked and poked in this manure pile. But somehow they missed stabbing the guys!

That must have been some big manure pile, that's all I can say. Lord knows where these guys were put. I always wondered how they managed to breathe. After the Germans left, the French farmer dug them out of the pile and they took off again into the woods.

It's possible that being Indian helped Wilbur to survive. He knew how to hunt and fish, he knew the cycles of the moon. He would have known how to survive and hide pretty well.

Finally, they found their way back to the American side and were safe. You'd think they'd send you home after an ordeal like that, but they just put him right back with his unit! They needed every man they could get.

Of course, I didn't know any of this at the time. I only knew he was missing.

Over the years, I wanted to ask him so many times what had happened but I left him alone about it. I could see that it was hard for all the men when they came home, getting back to their families and their jobs, making the adjustment from being in the war to living a quiet life, and it was obvious that Wilbur was traumatized more than many of the others.

There was one other problem we were dealing with: Wilbur

had trouble finding work when he got back from overseas. We were shocked to find out that some people in town were angry at him. I mean, people of color—black people, Indian people—folks who had been friendly with him before he left but were bent out of shape because he'd been in the "white" army. They thought he had been trying to pass for white!

You know, with people like that, you don't always get a chance to explain yourself. It wasn't Wilbur's fault that he was put in the white army. When he reported for duty, he told them he was Indian. It was the army that put him in the white army, not the Negro army. Wilbur wasn't trying to put on airs or act like he was better. It was out of his hands. But there were people who held it against him.

And so my husband had trouble finding a job. He realized he'd have to work for himself. So on top of everything else, he had to start his own business. He was already a good carpenter and had built lots of small houses, including ours, so it seemed like the best thing to do. But it makes me sad to this day that some people in town shut him out like that.

10

There was something else we had to contend with, even after the war. The Ku Klux Klan was after us.

Most people think the KKK only went after black people, and only in the South. Not so! They were up here in the northern states, too. And they went after anybody—anybody who was different. We were all put in the same category as far as the Klan was concerned. We never knew when they would go by our house and shoot at us or make some other kind of trouble.

They knew we were Indian. Heck, they knew exactly who we were. And we knew who they were, too! But there wasn't a doggone thing we could do about it. They were the people in power. They were the lawyers, the business owners, and so on. They were the big wheels in town. They "owned" Bridgeton, you might say. But there were also some country folk, white, of course, who were part of it, too, including some right down the road here.

From the time I was a little girl, I was taught to watch out for the Klan. They used to meet right down the road from here. It's a church now. Back in the twenties and thirties, they would put on a red light and that was some kind of signal that they were going to gather. My mom would say, "Any time you see

that red light on, you kids come in the house, don't stay outdoors and play. Because you don't know what they're going to
do." We would have to come in the house and just sit quietly on
the couch, maybe read or something, until they went away.

Well, time had passed, I had my own children to worry
about, and the Klan was still making trouble for us. On one
particular day, Wilbur's sister, Margaret, and her husband,
Blake, called us up on the phone. Blake said, "Stay away
from the front of your house!" And I said, "What's going on?"
He said, "Well, they just shot at your aunt Mary's store, and
Rhoda's picture window, they shot that out, too." And he said
they were coming down the road here, this way.

Wilbur and his brother, Jesse, and the other Indian men
were fed up. They decided they were not going to let us be sitting ducks. This was in about 1947, and they were all back
from the war. They were veterans! They were not going to put
up with this stuff anymore. So they all got together with their
rifles and shotguns and hid behind bushes on the side of the
road, waiting for these KKK guys to come along.

In the middle of all this, a young couple was driving by and
they had a flat tire, right out front here. They were a white couple, probably from Philadelphia, heading to the shore. So my
brother-in-law Jesse popped out from behind the bushes and
said, "Can we help you?" He forgot he and the other men had
these guns in their hands. And the girl in the car, she was scared
half to death.

Well my brother-in-law and my husband set about fixing
that tire. That's the way we do things. Always help a stranger
that's stranded. And they got that tire fixed and that poor young

couple couldn't wait to get out of there. I guess you could say it was not a good time or place to get a flat tire!

While all this was going on, the Klan guys did not show up. We think they saw all the commotion, and that our men had rifles and all, so they backed down. But sometime during the night they built a small cross and set it afire, directly across from my brother-in-law's house. I can still see the spot from my front window!

People say that terrorism—with the Oklahoma City bombing and the World Trade Center and all—is something new in this country. Not so. For people of color, terrorism has been going on for a long, long time.

PART V

A "Working" Mother

On her way to work: Marion "Strong Medicine"
Gould, circa 1952.

THE SMELL OF GINGER wafts through the air of Marion Strong Medicine's bungalow. It's a beautiful day in the fall, and since early that morning she has baked dozens of cookies—a type of ginger cookie she calls "crybabies"—for her son Billy's birthday. She needs to make "extra," she explains, for her other son, Mark, the Chief. She does the reverse on Mark's birthday, making sure that Billy gets his "fair share."

Both men are in their sixties. Some things don't change.

Marion Strong Medicine is known to be a good cook and baker. She is famous in the tribe for her macaroni and cheese, to which she adds her own secret ingredients. She also makes a delicious succotash, an American Indian favorite.

These days, however, with the exception of the crybabies on her sons' birthdays, she is cooking for one. Gone are the days when she worked outside the home, purchased the groceries as she left work, hurried home, and cooked enormous meals for her family.

Although the postwar years are typically thought of as a time when American women stayed home and raised chil-

Women workers at a sewing factory, Bridgeton, New Jersey, circa 1955. Marion "Strong Medicine" Gould is standing at far left.

dren, and men were the wage earners, this was not an option for many women of color. Women such as Marion Strong Medicine had little choice but to work outside the home. Because men of color had a harder time finding work than white men did, and often weren't paid at the same level as their white counterparts, a woman's income was needed to make ends meet.

Many of the jobs held by women of color fell into the category of what was thought of as "women's work," such as sewing, waitressing, or housecleaning. Typically, these jobs were physically demanding, low-paying, and not particularly pleasant. No doubt many of these women would rather

The Gould family home, at right, as it looked in the 1950s
when the street on which it was located was still a dirt road.
Built by Wilbur Gould for his bride in the early 1940s,
it is now the home of elder son, Billy Gould.

have been raising their children at home. In Lenape culture,
women traditionally looked after children while collecting
wild plants for food and tending gardens; men hunted and
fished.

In Marion Strong Medicine's case, her family needed the
income but, at the same time, she came to enjoy working
outside the home. The support she received from the Indian
community, where everyone has a hand in raising children,
is part of what made this possible.

11

Once the war was over, there weren't a lot of jobs available to women. The men came home and they were rehired to do the jobs that women had been doing. Jobs like the one I had at the Birds Eye plant were suddenly gone.

So I got a job working part time in a laundry. It was the worst job I ever had.

I never did like the heat, and there's nothing hotter than a laundry. But the worst part was the bedbugs. I have a deep fear of bedbugs. It stems from an incident when Wilbur was in the army and I went to visit one of his uncles in Camden. Wilbur's uncle says to me, "I'm going to take care of the boys. You go ahead and go to the movies. You deserve time to yourself." So off I go to the theater. When I got back, I hear the boys whimpering in their sleep and I thought to myself, I wonder why they're squirming and carrying on. So I went in there and turned the light on, and the whole ceiling was covered with these little red bugs! I mean solid!

When I was growing up, we never had bedbugs in our house. I remember how my mom made us go outside and play, and she would burn sulfur candles. My mom was fastidious.

Anyway, there I am, working in this laundry, and just

amazed at how many people brought in linens that had bedbugs in 'em. And I'm talking about linens that belonged mostly to rich people. I spent the whole day worrying that one of those doggone bugs was going to get on me.

My next job was at a sewing factory. This was in 1947. By then, Wilbur was getting his construction business going, but we needed my income. Besides, I loved going to work, making some money, just being part of things other than being at home. Because I worked, we were able to buy our first new car. Oh, how I loved that car. Can't for the life of me remember what it was, only that it was silver-gray, loaded with chrome, and had an enormous engine. When you put your foot to the metal, that thing would move.

One time Wilbur referred to it as "his" car and I said, "What?! Wait a minute! It's more mine than it is yours! We wouldn't have it if I didn't make the money to buy it." Well, he had to agree this was true. So I drove it most of the time, to work. Anyway, he had a pickup truck that made more sense for his construction work.

The sewing factory was in downtown Bridgeton. We made "dress-up" dresses and lots of sports outfits—like the kind women wore when they played golf. We had different customers, and depending on who they were, we used better quality material and wider seams. For instance, Montgomery Ward ordered clothes with three-quarter-inch seams, while some other stores wanted one-quarter-inch, which is skimpy. If you want to know the quality of a dress you're buying, look at the seams.

At first I was hired to be a presser. I worked on a machine

where you could flatten a large piece of material. I also worked with an iron—we called it "slinging an iron." I remember that I got paid twenty-five or twenty-six dollars a week.

I hoped to work on a sewing machine because it was more pleasant, plus you could make more money—you got paid by the bundle, so if you worked fast, you could make more money. Most of the women who were pressers or slung an iron were black. The women who worked on the sewing machines were white.

After a while, I persuaded the owner to put me on a machine. His name was Mr. Bernard, and he was a Jewish man from New York. He was a nice person, and he gave me a chance.

Working on a sewing machine was downright fun by comparison. And I made friends with women I would never have gotten to know otherwise. We used to go to lunch, and sometimes we'd do errands together. Sometimes we went shoe shopping.

I think some of these white gals learned a little bit about the Indian way, just from being around me. One time we were walking down the street together and I saw a young woman in tears. She was going into a store with two small children who were acting up. I didn't know her. But I told the girls I was with, "Wait a second," and I went over to the young woman and talked soothingly to the children. I distracted them and calmed them down. It gave the mom a chance to catch her breath.

The girls who were with me were surprised. They said, "Marion, do you know her?" They thought it was odd that I would bother getting involved in a situation like that when I didn't know the woman. But that's part of the Indian way. If you see a mother who is overwhelmed, you don't judge, you don't criticize. You just step up and be helpful.

After I'd been on a sewing machine for a while, Mr. Bernard decided he could trust me, and he gave me some new responsibilities. I was good at keeping track of things, and I like to be organized. This is very important in a factory, especially where you're making all these dresses that look the same, only some are better quality than others.

One day Mr. Bernard said he wanted to put me in charge of the guys who cut the material. And I said, "Mr. Bernard, I like what I'm doing." But he said, "Yeah, but I think you'll like this better. And I know I can trust you."

Well, there was this one guy who was out to get me. He didn't like me for love nor money. He didn't like me for nothing! I used to fill in wherever I was needed, if we were short for some reason—say, someone called in sick or we had a rush order. This one time, they needed me on a sewing machine, putting the top and bottom of a dress together at the waistline.

When I went in the next day, I had this whole heap of dresses and I could see right away they weren't mine. The tops of dresses that were supposed to be small were sewed together with ones that were larger! I knew I hadn't done that. Besides, my initials weren't on the back.

Well, you see, somebody screwed 'em up on purpose. There was nothing I could do, except when Mr. Bernard came I went straight up to him. I took this whole armful of dresses, I took the slip that I had written on the day before—you didn't get paid *unless you had those—and I brought it all up to him and I said, "Mr. Bernard, I don't know what's going on, but if you look at the back of the tags on the dress, you'll find that my initials aren't on there."*

Mr. Bernard figured out pretty quickly what had happened. He said, "Just leave those dresses here, and you go on back to your machine." And that's what I did. First thing you know, Mr. Bernard was having it out with the old guy who set me up. He really got called on the carpet. I don't think Mr. Bernard fired him, but at least he was told to leave me alone.

The factory was located over an auto dealership, but after a few years we moved around the corner to a different building where we had more space. Everything was going along fine, but then I started having trouble from this one woman. I forget what her name was, but she was a bitchy person, and she didn't want nothing to do with anybody of color.

There was a secretary named Mary and one day she told me, "Marion, I have something to tell you." It seems that this woman—I'll call her Miss Bigot—she was running her mouth behind my back and telling people that she could not work for me, that she would not answer to a woman of color.

So, Mary went and told Mr. Bernard. He came out of his office and asked all the girls, "Are you making sure that you're putting all your information on the slips? Because they have to be turned in before you go home tonight, so Marion can count them." And that's when he heard Miss Bigot say, "I'm not going to have nobody colored tell me what to do."

So Mr. Bernard said, "Well, if Marion doesn't okay them, you won't get paid." Oh, my goodness, she was calling me all kind of names, according to Mary. Finally Mr. Bernard said, "If you don't want to work here with Marion, you can go on home and never come back." Well, she must have needed the job because she came back. But we never heard another peep out of her again.

To this day, I don't know if she knew I was Indian or what. She just saw I had brown skin and decided not to like me. When I think about that woman, I wonder what kind of upbringing she had. Someone taught her to think that way.

I had one other problem at the sewing factory, and that was when Mr. Bernard brought in a young partner. Well, this guy was the kind of boss who expected you to kiss his butt. When you come in, he expected you to stop and pay a whole lot of attention to him, but I'd just say hi and go about my business. I got right to work.

But this one day, as I was coming down to my particular area, he said, "You can't speak to me, can you?" And I said, "I was brought up for a man to speak first, and the woman to speak afterwards."

Well, he followed me around the corner. He was just bugging the heck out of me. And I very nicely said, "Aw, go to hell," under my breath. But I said it too loud. Oh! He was so mad. He said, "I'm going to get rid of you!" and I said very calmly, "You are? You better go and tell Mr. Bernard." He said, "I don't have to tell him anything. I'm going to get rid of you!"

They had bought this new machine that made tags. I didn't have to do the work, but it was part of my job, once the stuff was bundled properly, to make sure the tags were put on correctly.

So I said, "Well, what are you going to do about this machine? Who's going to be responsible for it?" He said, "Don't worry about it! I'll get rid of the machine!" And I thought to myself, "Well, if that isn't the dumbest thing I ever heard. The man is supposed to be the boss, he's supposed to have brains, and he comes off like this?" I wanted to laugh out loud so bad but I didn't dare.

Well, Mr. Bernard heard the commotion, and he came back there. He asked what was wrong and the guy said to him, "That bitch, I can't make her do anything." And Mr. Bernard said, "Well, that's not your job. Leave her alone."

So I had the last laugh. But it makes you wonder, What is it about human beings that there is always someone who's trying to pick on the others? They're trying to make themselves the top dog by putting someone else down. It might be because you're Indian, or black, or a foreigner, or a woman, or even just because you're old. But whatever the reason, you have to fight back, in my opinion. Always stand up to a bully—that's my philosophy!

12

There's a lot of talk today about women working outside the home, versus women staying at home to raise children. Nobody's sorted all that out yet. Which is better? I'd say it's very individual. Whatever works for a woman and her husband is the right way.

I was a "working mom," as they say, but I was used to the idea. My mom had to work. Women of color often didn't have many options. That's just the way it was.

I'll be the first one to say that I had help. A lot of help. My husband was a strong father. Wilbur didn't put up with any crap from our boys, and he spent time with them, teaching them how to fish and hunt, working on cars together, things like that. Of course, Wilbur was pretty useless in the kitchen—when he did cook something, you wouldn't want to eat it—but he was always there for our boys.

But the boys had all kinds of adults keeping an eye on them since we were pretty much related to everybody on this stretch of road. They would go over to my parents' house, which was a mile down the road. My sister, Dianne, was still living at home, and she looked after them a lot. Or the boys could go right next door to us, where Wilbur's father, Pop, lived, or to *their uncle Jesse's house on the other side of Pop, or Aunt Margaret's house on the other side of him. On the opposite side of us was where Aunt Isabel lived. And across the street was one of Wilbur's cousins.*

If one of the boys got in trouble, he'd already been punished by the time I heard about it. Somebody would have called or stopped by and told me all about it. And then Wilbur and I would give it to him all over again.

It wasn't like today when the parents defend their kid no matter how bad he is. You can't even swat your own kid—they call the government and have you arrested! I know it's not popular to think this way anymore, but I don't see what's wrong with swatting a kid on the fanny once in a while.

On weekends, I used to watch all the kids in the neighborhood. It was my way of making it up to some of the kinfolk who'd been keeping an eye on my rascals all week. I made all my own clothes, and I had my sewing room set up in the house so I could watch from the window. Kids are so funny! If they thought they did something wrong, first thing you know, they'd be peeking around the corner to see if I was looking out the window. They'd really give themselves away.

Kids will do the stupidest things sometimes. One year Wilbur got the boys BB guns for Christmas. I wasn't too happy about it but I kept my mouth shut to keep the peace. Well, one time I heard the BB guns going off upstairs—inside the house! And I raced up there and those two boys were shooting at something in the backyard—straight through the screens! They put holes in my screens! Oh, I was so mad. I said, "Didn't it occur to you that when the weather's warmer, the mosquitoes will get in? I hope they eat you alive! It'll serve you right!"

Sometimes the boys would try to scare me. Oh, how they loved to do that. It was a game we had. The screen door would open and in would poke this stick with a live snake dangling off it. To tell you the truth, I wasn't afraid of it. I'm really not afraid of anything. But the boys weren't satisfied unless I pretended to scream and screech and carry on. That was part of the fun. Those are some of my best memories, and I wouldn't trade 'em for anything.

I decided early on that I wanted my kids to explore their own interests and talents. As long as I could make them mind me, I didn't interfere much.

Kids had more freedom then. It's a shame kids are cooped up now the way they are. I'm not sure the world is really that much more dangerous. To some extent, yes. There are illegal drugs and gangs. But there were perverts back in the old days, too. When I was a girl, these men would come over from Philadelphia—their cars had Pennsylvania tags—and they'd try to grab girls walking on our country roads. The way I see it, there's always going to be perverts. What are you going to do? Keep your kids locked up forever?

Especially in the summertime, my kids were never home. They spent all their time playing outdoors, and they loved it. There was a stream across the road that leads out to the Cohansey River. Billy and Mark used to take my canning jars and take 'em down the road and scoop up the frogs and whatever else they could find.

Mark was eleven and Billy was twelve when I found out

that I was expecting a third child, which was something of a surprise but, hey, that's life. This was 1953, and I was thirty-one.

This time, I decided to have the baby in the hospital and not at home, like with the first two. I didn't have much choice because old Dr. Bacon had retired by then. It was a boy, and we named him Jared Jeffrey, though we always called him Jeff.

Well, I'll tell you what happened with Jeff. I was in the hospital for five days after he was born. I had the baby, they brang the baby, I got fed, and all that. But the doctor didn't remember I was there!

Finally, I got a nurse to help me out. I said, "You know what? The doctor has had me in here forever. I want to go home!" Well, she went and got him and he finally showed up and he told me, "Marion, I'm sorry, I forgot all about you."

So that was my introduction to modern medicine!

Once I got home, I had to think about working again. Mr. Bernard wanted me back at the factory, so he let me bring the baby with me. So I had Jeff in a little bassinet, right next to me. I don't remember if the other women were allowed to do that, but nobody seemed to think anything of it. And why not? Indian women always carried their babies with them while they did their work. It's not really any different, except I couldn't keep the baby on my back like Indian women did in the old days.

Billy and Mark were very proud to be big brothers. In fact, they tried to be helpful to me. Sometimes their attempts at being helpful made things worse, but if they were trying to do something nice, they didn't get punished. To Indians, intentions are very important. If somebody decides they want to do something to help you, you don't browbeat 'em if they mess up.

For instance, when they were in junior high school, about the time Jeff was a baby, Mark and Billy used to get this idea they were going to make cakes after school—one to eat right away, and one as a present to me. Well, I was a working mom, I'd come home from work, and the last thing I need is a cake. But the boys were so proud. They'd say, "Look, Mom, look what we made you!" And they'd cleaned up—all the dishes were washed and everything put away.

But then I'd wait until they were out of the kitchen. I'd check my eggs, and sure enough, they used twice as many eggs as you're supposed to! It was annoying, but what are you going to do? The kids come home from school and they all had a bottomless pit. They were always hungry. I figured, as long as they're not burning the house down, you have to let 'em do something, you have to let them experiment. You can't control their every move. And you don't pull your hair out over a couple of eggs.

Sometimes Billy and Mark would help me with the laundry, too. If I had clothes down the cellar that didn't get washed yet, sometimes they'd decide, "Mom needs some help—we'll wash her clothes for her." And they would even try to iron my clothes for me. I dreaded it sometimes, but most of the time it worked out all right. Every once in a while they would ruin one of my blouses, but I didn't get on their backs about it. I let them do what they had planned to do.

I wanted my children to be happy. I wanted them to enjoy their lives. When Billy and Mark were in their teens, they had dance parties at our house. Wilbur would roll back the rug so they had a dance floor. They'd play rock 'n' roll records—Elvis and all that fun stuff. I encouraged it. I made food for them, and they'd set up the records and the record player, and they'd dance until the wee hours. Wilbur and I would be upstairs— our bedroom was directly over the living room—and Wilbur could sleep right through it, but I couldn't. I didn't mind, though.

Billy and Mark were very close—they still are—but they had altogether different ways of reacting when they got in trouble. Mark would just admit it. When his daddy would ask him, "Why did you do that?" Mark would say, "Because I wanted to." Well, that used to drive Wilbur nuts. It made him more angry.

Now, Billy was just the opposite. He tried to work things out so that he didn't get blamed for it. So Mark probably got the blame for a lot of things that Billy did. At least, that's what I'm thinking now.

As Jeff got a little older he became just like Billy and Mark—always up to something. Jeff used to hang around with Harry, one of the cousins who was about the same age. And, of course, they got into some trouble together.

One day I was home and I heard a noise coming from under the house. I went down in the cellar, and there was Jeff and Harry, drinking my cherry wine. They tried to be sneaky but they weren't too smart about it. They were only eight or nine years old, and they didn't realize that when you take the juice out and leave the cherries, there would be a couple of inches of liquid missing from the jar.

I didn't whip their behinds, though. I just told them not to do it again. Out of their earshot, I kind of laughed about it. It seemed like normal kid stuff to me. But I didn't let them know that.

All three of our sons definitely had a different personality, but they had a few things in common. All three of them were curious. They would try anything once—well, maybe more than once.

But those three stuck together like glue. It didn't make any difference what was going on, if the boys had any idea that my husband and I were having any problem with anything, they would get their heads together. They wouldn't tell us a popeyed thing, but they would monitor us like we were kids! That's what they would do. They were protective. They respected us as their Elders, but they wanted to be sure that Mom and Dad were okay. That's the way they were brought up. That's the Indian way. Family was family and they stuck together.

I am proud of my sons, the way they turned out. They are not the kind of people who waste time and get paid for it. They're honest, kindhearted, and they persevere, and those are the qualities that matter most to me.

PART VI

Changing Times

THE 1950s AND EARLY 1960s were a devastating time for Native Americans, an "all-time low for tribal existence on this continent," as Charles Wilkinson, a law professor and expert on Indian rights, states in his book *Blood Struggle: The Rise of Modern Indian Nations*.

Statistics cited by Wilkinson and others are stunning. They include an infant mortality rate for Native Americans that was five times the national average; a life expectancy twenty-five years shorter; and unemployment as high as 90 percent for some tribes.

While all Indians suffered from discrimination, those who lived on reservations were at the mercy of the Bureau of Indian Affairs, which controlled their basic freedoms, including what language they could speak (English) and what they could wear (Western clothes).

In 1953, Congress passed a resolution that would create further damage. Known as the "termination policy," it was meant to force Indians living on reservations—then about 85 percent of the Indian population, and by 1990, less than 30 percent—to assimilate into the American mainstream.

Funds were cut off, lands ended up being sold, and a large segment of America's indigenous people were abruptly abandoned.

Native Americans who were not living on reservations, such as Marion Strong Medicine and her family, watched events unfold with sadness and trepidation. They understood that the government's treatment of Indians on reservations was symptomatic of society's view of native people in general. While it was a particularly grim era for Native Americans, it was at the same time an era of great progress for black Americans. The black civil rights movement, led by the Reverend Dr. Martin Luther King Jr. and others, was capturing the attention of the nation. As Marion Strong Medicine remembers it, the success of that movement provided some much-needed hope and inspiration to Native Americans.

Ironically, the success of the black civil rights movement seemed to alter the long-standing relationship between some blacks and Indians, at least temporarily. Marion Strong Medicine recalls new tensions about skin color, a new twist in the tragic saga of race relations in America.

13

I remember being excited and inspired by the black civil rights movement. When Rosa Parks's photo was in the newspaper after she refused to go to the back of the bus, I was thrilled. I thought, "Good for you!"

Black people and Indians have a lot in common. For a long time, we were both lumped into one category. We were both considered "beneath" white people in every way.

The relationship between black people and Indians goes back a long time in this country. Some slaves who escaped and headed north were helped by Indians. Part of the Underground Railroad went right through Lenape territory. Our tribe was among the people who helped to hide and feed escaped slaves. If they wanted to stay with our tribe, that was fine, too.

A lot of people don't realize this but at one time, Indians—including my tribe, the Lenape—were made into slaves. This was back in the 1600s, when Europeans first got here. The white people gave up on it, though, because Indians ran away. It was very different for black people—they were so far away from their people, and their way of life, that it was much harder for them to survive if they escaped. If you don't know the terrain, or even what plants to eat, how are you going to live?

"STRONG MEDICINE" SPEAKS

I sometimes wonder where white people got the idea they're above everyone else. Supposedly, white people came from "advanced" cultures, but I think that all depends on how you look at it.

For example, going way back, white colonists didn't think very much of our gardens. They planted everything in perfect rows, and to them, our gardens looked like a mess. But we did this on purpose, planting in alternating rows so when the corn grew tall, the stalks provided a stake for the pumpkin or squash vines to grow onto. It didn't look pretty to white people's eyes, but it made perfect sense. See, they could have learned something if they hadn't been so quick to judge.

So this was the attitude we had to contend with. Europeans thought they knew better than anyone else. Black people were dragged here in chains and made into slaves. Indian people were driven off their land and killed outright. So the Indians and the blacks, we understood each other.

Then, in the 1950s, comes the black civil rights movement, and people like me—and my husband, and my kids—all of a sudden we aren't dark enough. Black people didn't want anything to do with us anymore. At least, that's the way it was here in Bridgeton. You had to be black. Indian was not black.

We were totally left out in the cold. The worst part is what it was doing to the kids. We talked to our boys about it, because they were very upset. They were getting attacked on their way to school. I was worried that someone was going to get seriously hurt or killed because my sons fought back. It's in their nature.

I remember saying to Mark, "Well, if someone doesn't like you because of the color of your skin—either you're too light for black folks, or too dark for white folks—to heck with them. There's not a thing you can do about it except go about your business. You can't change people like that. Just go ahead and live your life."

So that's what it was like around here. We felt pushed aside—or maybe left behind—by the black civil rights movement. At the same time, their success made us realize we needed to do the same. We were inspired by it, definitely. It's just a sin and a shame that we were divided in the process of moving forward. Fortunately, that rift pretty much healed in time.

One problem Indians had was that we didn't have the national leadership that black people did. There was no Indian Rosa Parks or Indian Martin Luther King. Not anyone at that level, who was a household name. We also weren't as united as black people seemed to be, and I think we realized we needed to get organized—not just within each tribe, but all tribes working together.

I could only hope, in the back of my mind, that somehow Indians would find a way to move forward, too. By the 1950s and early '60s, I would say our tribe was in danger of disappearing altogether, yet I had some hope. I could see stirrings in the next generation—my sons' generation. We were still a hidden people, but one thing was obvious. The younger generation wasn't going to take it anymore.

Two sisters, two different paths: Marion "Strong Medicine" Gould (CENTER) with her sister, Dianne (FAR LEFT), and their mother (FAR RIGHT). Marion Strong Medicine married within the tribe, and her children were raised as Native American. Dianne's husband was black, and her children were raised as African American. In this photo from 1953, Marion "Strong Medicine" Gould is holding her infant son Jeff. Her son Billy is standing second from left. Mark, the future Chief, is crouched below him. Dianne's children in this photo are Davy (FAR LEFT, front row) and Susan (FAR RIGHT, front row).

14

Now, all this stuff is going on, black people are moving forward, Indian people started to get little glimmers of hope. But my life, on a personal level, was changing, too.

I was always very close to my mom. She had got tired of working at home as a seamstress and wanted to get hired at the sewing factory, and I was really happy. It meant that I would get to see her all day long.

Everything went along fine for a while. Then, all of a sudden, she wasn't up to it. Finally, she told us she had cancer of the pancreas. This was 1963, and there wasn't much that could be done for her.

I think she was sick a lot longer than she let on. I look back at this picture I have of her, and I think now—there's a certain look in her eyes—that she was already leaving us. Once I found out how sick she was, I quit my job to take care of her. I'd been working at the sewing factory for sixteen years, since 1947.

I pretty much moved back home with Mom and Daddy because she kept asking for me, day and night. She wouldn't let anyone else touch her. I had two aunts who would come and help spell me. They would come over and sit with her so that I could take a breather, or get organized. But most of the time it was just me at her bedside, 'cause that's what Mom wanted. Daddy pretty much fell apart, and Mom seemed to think my little sister, Dianne, was too young to handle the situation. Poor Dianne, she was in her thirties and had a husband and four children, but in Mom's mind she was still a little kid.

Dianne is quiet and introverted—the opposite of me! She took a different path in life than me. She didn't marry Indian. She married a black man, and her children were raised, more or less, as black. Not that it made any difference, because it didn't. She and her family lived over in Vineland, and Dianne stayed very close to my parents.

So Dianne was there, trying to help, but Mom was acting like she was still a baby. Every time I laid down to rest and go to sleep, even if Dianne or my aunts were there, Mom would call my name. Finally, I just took a quilt and put it on the floor beside her bed. As long as I slept there, she was all right.

The only time I went home to Wilbur was to take a shower and change my clothes. By this time, Billy and Mark had left home—both of them had served in the military; coincidentally, they were both stationed at the same time in Korea, where the U.S. kept troops although the Korean War was long over.

So my husband was alone with Jeff, who was nine or ten years old then. Of course, it was just a mile down the road from my parents' house. Wilbur had lost his own mother when he was a little boy, so he understood what I was going through. Besides, this is what Indians do. Even if we could have afforded it, why would I hire someone else to look after my mother?

Overseas: Billy (LEFT) and Mark, the future Chief,
in the armed forces in Korea, circa 1961.

Mom was suffering so I had mixed feelings when she died. I felt a little relieved that it was over for her, but I missed her terribly. I think it took me at least two years to get over it, to the extent you ever get over it.

After Mom died, I had my hands full with Daddy. He lived another fourteen years without her. He retired from the Post Office in Philadelphia and was at home all the time. Oh, he was a pain in the butt as he got older. He had four girlfriends, all at the same time!

Sometimes Daddy would drink too much, and one time he left the house wearing only his hat. I said, "Daddy, what are you doing?" He said, "What do you mean?" And I said, "You're buck naked." He hadn't even noticed. It was a good thing I was there that day to make him go back in the house and put some pants on.

Mark Gould in his high school
graduation photo, 1960.

*At the same time, I was helping with Wilbur's dad, too.
"Pop" lived right next door to me and Wilbur, in the house
where I'm living now, and he was almost as difficult as my
dad. I don't know what gets into these old men when they outlive their wives, but they don't do all that well. Margaret, my
sister-in-law, brought Pop some succotash one time. When she
visited again, he tried to give it back to her. She looked in the
fridge and there wasn't a thing in it.*

*After that, Pop came over to our house to eat, or I went over
there every day to make sure he was eating. He would say,
"Marion, play me some music. Sing to me." My mom had me
take piano lessons for two or three years as a girl, and I always
loved to play, and sing, too. So I would sit at the little organ*

and play the music he liked. I guess you'd call it hillbilly music. He'd be sitting there, in his recliner, with his feet up. And when I'd finish playing and singing, I'd turn around and look at him and he would be laying there with tears streaming down his face. Oh, these old men, they get sentimental! And they are a handful!

It's the circle of life, though. You start out as a baby and you are totally dependent. Then you grow up and raise the next generation. If you live long enough, you'll be needing your young people to give you a hand, just as you held out your hand to them when they were little. The way that Indians look at it, it's the most natural thing in the world. It's not something to be afraid of. It's life.

After Pop died, it seemed like everybody in the family lived in his house at one time or another. Every one of our nieces and nephews who got married ended up living here for several months, until they got themselves together so they could find their own place. As soon as one would go, here comes somebody else, asking, "Aunt Marion, can we stay in Pop's old house for a while?" And I'd think, "Okay, here we go again!" But we never said no, and nobody ever outstayed their welcome.

We aren't all that possessive about our houses. Why, Billy and his wife are living in the house that Wilbur built when he and I were first married and raised the boys. We sold the house to Billy and built another house across the street. Later, we sold that house to one of Wilbur's cousins, and moved into Pop's old house.

You know, this is really not all that different than the way the Lenape lived a long time ago. They built these things called longhouses, structures made out of branches and covered with tree bark. Sometimes they had four or five related families living in one—as many as twenty-five people, or so I've been told. Here we are, in the twenty-first century, practically doing the same thing.

The only one in my family who left home for a long time was my brother, Boyer. He had served in the army during World War II, and after he was discharged, he enrolled in college in Alabama and got married.

Well, Boyer's story is a very sad one. He started getting these terrible headaches. He went to an army hospital and all they would give him was aspirin. Well, that was only the beginning of his troubles. The next thing you know he's back in the hospital again, only this time the doctors are saying he's crazy.

When we heard that, I said to my sister, Dianne, "Listen, we've got to go down there and see what this is all about." So we took my and Wilbur's car—I think it was a big Buick—and we drove ourselves to Alabama.

When we got there, we found out that Boyer wasn't crazy at all. He was in a lot of pain, and they finally diagnosed him with multiple sclerosis. He was still a young man, only in his late twenties at the time.

I told his wife, "Look, why don't you just get everything all packed up, I'll help you, and we'll go north." So that's what we did. I had hoped that she and Boyer would come back to Bridgeton with us, but her people lived in Chattanooga, and she decided that's as far as they were going to go.

I sometimes think Boyer got sick because he'd been away from home for so long. I have this idea that when people move far from where they were born and raised, they are more vulnerable to all kinds of sicknesses. I think you build immunity very early and then it's a shock to the body to live elsewhere. Maybe it's one of the reasons some of the Indians who were moved to reservations have so many health problems.

I don't remember how much time passed, but Boyer and his wife eventually did come home to Bridgeton. He was really struggling by then. He had one hand that he couldn't use at all. He kept getting worse, and he ended up in a wheelchair. They lived here for a few years, but then he felt he couldn't get the medical care he needed here, so he and his wife decided to move to Washington, D.C.

When he lived in Washington, I kept in touch with him by phone. He would call me every week and we would chat for a long time. We'd talk about something that interested us— usually, something involving psychology, and why people think and act in a certain way—and in between calls we would look things up. It was like a little game we had. He thought because he had gone to college he could one-up me, but I liked to surprise him. I had a set of encyclopedias, and if I couldn't find the information there I would go to a bookstore or library and get it. Oh, it was fun. It was our little competition.

Boyer did his best to live well despite being so ill. He decided to study accounting and was very excited about it. He was supposed to start studying with a professor who was going to come to the house, but then he took sick and ended up in the hospital. It was around that time when they had that flu coming from

Asia, and he got that. And then one of the young ministers that he was friends with, he called me. He told me that Boyer had passed away. This was 1968. Boyer was forty-two years old.

I still miss Mom and Boyer, and I'm sure I will until the day I leave this world. I wish they had lived to see the changes that were surely coming for the Indian people, but it was not to be.

15

After Mom died, I didn't want to go back to work at the sewing factory. It seemed like it was time for something new. I started thinking about going to college, maybe studying to become a teacher.

I was in my forties, and I was a grandma now. Both Billy and Mark had married and had little ones of their own. My first grandchild, Mark's daughter Tyrese, was born in 1963. We call her Ty.

But it seemed like there just wasn't enough of me to go around. Wilbur needed me, Jeff needed me—it seemed like everybody did. So I put everyone else first. I didn't go to college.

In the end, I found a way to compromise. I heard they needed substitute teachers over at Gouldtown School, where my husband had gone to grammar school, so I applied, and they hired me. I loved working there. I did this for several years in the mid-1960s.

But, oh! Talk about changing times. I couldn't believe how much children had changed since my boys were little. Or I should say, how much child rearing had changed.

I was just amazed at how the children behaved, and how

Tyrese "Brightflower" Gould, Mark's
daughter, and the first of Marion and
Wilbur's grandchildren, circa 1966.

*they were being treated at home. They were white, Indian,
black, whatever. That area, Gouldtown, used to be all Indian
but it had changed.*

*A lot of the kids were being raised in homes where the par-
ents had split up. These children did not have the kind of
extended family that I had, and my kids had. Some of them did
just fine, but quite a few of them had problems from their home
life that carried over into their schoolwork.*

*Usually I substituted for teachers who taught reading to
kids who were labeled "slow." Some of them really were a little slow, but mostly, I would say they were neglected. Nobody
at home had taught them right from wrong, or read to them, or*

spent any time explaining anything to them. A few of them weren't "slow" at all, they were sick and had been lumped in with these other kids. Half a dozen or more had sickle-cell anemia.

Although I was only a substitute, I took the job seriously. I put my heart into it and I found it very rewarding. I had all kinds of kids who would come looking for me at school, and they weren't even in my classes. They'd come up to me and say, "Mrs. Gould, can I talk to you?" and I'd say, "What's wrong? What kind of problem have you got today?" They just needed someone to listen to them. And I loved being there for them.

There was one boy who was about thirteen, and one day he said, "My parents told me to get out." I said, "What do you mean, 'get out'?" And he said, "They told me I had to get out of the house, unless my grades come up."

Well, I thought that was terrible. I started paying more attention to him. I'd ask him, "Who gets you up in the morning, helps you get ready for school?" or "What happens to you, after you go home from school?" I took notes on all these things and made sure all the other teachers knew about it. And, fortunately, they went along with me, and we took things like that to the principal.

Another boy kept saying, "My parents don't love me, they don't like me." One time he said, "I don't always get something to eat." So, you know, these kinds of things, they tear you up, but you have to try to deal with it. These kids had to depend on some of the people in school because their parents didn't want to be bothered with 'em.

I had different kinds of programs for the kids, depending on what their problems were. One time I got really annoyed at some of the boys because there was a little girl who was trying really hard to read, and they would make fun of her, just ridicule her. Finally, I sat down and told them all a story. I said, "Once upon a time there was a little girl who was trying really hard to read, but some really bad, bad boys were making fun of her. They were so mean to her that it made her cry. And she was actually very smart, and very wise, but the boys wouldn't give her a chance. After a while she realized that they were a bunch of no-good hoodlums and she didn't let it stop her. She became the best reader in the class."

Those boys got very quiet listening to my story. It dawned on them that I was talking about them and so they saw it from a different perspective. And the little girl felt like somebody in this world was sticking up for her! So she was the hero of my story. The boys left her alone after that and the little girl did learn to read very well.

At least in those days we could discipline the kids who were bad, not like today. You can't yell at the bad ones today, let alone spank them. I don't know how these poor teachers do it. They have a tough row to hoe.

I think there are some trends that started in the sixties that have gotten out of hand. Somewhere along the line, some parents allowed themselves to get weak. A lot of people give in to their children.

The other day I saw a couple on a TV show, and the man was trying to discipline the children but the woman was just the opposite. They were almost broke, but the woman had bought her little daughter a ring that the girl had asked for. The husband was upset. But the mother said, "Well, I can't say no to her all the time."

And I thought, Lord, have mercy! It's your job, as a parent, to say no. I wonder why some parents are so worried about whether their kids like 'em or not? Hey, it's not a popularity contest. It's parenting. Sure, at times they're going to hate you. So what! They'll love you anyway.

Another thing that really knocked me over was when someone told me that some mothers today cook different meals for their kids, depending on what the children want to eat. When I heard that I said, "Are they kidding?" If I were

Marion "Strong Medicine" Gould with granddaughters
Shannon (LEFT) and Tyrese (RIGHT), circa 1978.
The girls are Mark Gould's daughters.

one of those mothers, I'd say, "Either eat what I cook, or starve!"

Let me tell you a story. When my granddaughter Ty was a teenager, she asked me how to make a blouse. After supper, I got the materials out, and I showed her how to do it, where to pin it, and how wide to make the seams. It was one of those kind that had a collar on it like a man's collar. Well, while I was doing something else she went ahead and sewed it. Then she came and showed it to me, and it was completely uneven. I said, "Ty, you can't wear that blouse like that!" She said, "Why not? I just got done making it." And I said, "I'm sorry, you're not going to wear it. You can do a better job than that."

I told her to rip that collar out. She said, "Oh, Nana, I don't want to do that. It'll look all right. I'll put a necktie on." I said, "No, you're not going to wear that blouse at all unless you're going to sew it properly. I'm not going to let you get away with sewing things wrong."

It was around ten o'clock, and I went to bed. The next morning when I got up, she said, "Nana, I think I got it pinned just right; will you look at it so I can sew this on?" She had ripped out the collar and was doing it over again. I sat there with her while she finished it, and finished it right.

Now, see, that's what you have to do with young people. You have to keep after 'em. You have to let 'em know that you expect certain things from them. All these things, like sewing a blouse properly, they carry over into everyday life.

I spent a lot of time with Ty and all my grandchildren when they were growing up. Ty and I are still especially close—she has five children of her own now, and lives about three miles *away. If you ask me how many grandchildren I have altogether, well, that's easy: I have six. As for great-grandchildren, I always have to stop and count. I think I'm up to thirteen. Almost all of them live nearby.*

I realize that a lot of people don't have family living nearby like that anymore. I think that's the root of a lot of problems. People don't have kinfolk they can lean on. The generations, in particular, are separated. Grandma and Grandpa have retired to Florida, say, and everyone else is scattered to the winds.

This is something that is very American, very modern, but Indian people try hard to reject it. We are a tribe. Oh, we have our disagreements. People don't always get along. But we know who we are. The world around us is in motion, and we adapt to it, but deep down we are still the same. That is one thing that has not changed.

A typical house, circa 1900, in an area known as Burden's Hill, where Marion "Strong Medicine" Gould's maternal ancestors resided. The style of house was favored by the Lenni-Lenape. This one was owned by one of Marion "Strong Medicine" Gould's relatives.

PART VII

A Woman's World

I HAVEN'T BEEN OVER here in a long time," Marion Strong Medicine says in a contemplative, faraway voice. We are in downtown Quinton, New Jersey, seventeen miles west of her home on the outskirts of Bridgeton.

Quinton, in Salem County, is where her mother was born in 1898. As a matriarchal society, who your mother was, and where she came from, is most important.

Marion Strong Medicine shows me where many Lenape Indians lived, in the area known as Burden's Hill. They favored a distinctive style of house: small wood-framed buildings that were taller than they were wide. The one where her mother was born and raised is long gone.

She reminisces about her visits to this area as a child. Most vivid in her memory is Uncle Frank, the one who wore his straight, black hair so long he could sit on it.

But Uncle Frank, and so many others, are long gone. The country cemeteries are filled with tombstones, some dating back several hundred years, that mark the graves of her extended family. Back in the woods, far from churches, are much older Lenape burial grounds. Because of grave robbers looking for Indian artifacts, members of the tribe are reluctant to disclose their location.

The lack of respect for Indian burial sites is a painful problem, and a national one. For the Lenape, the issue exploded in 2001 when they were informed by an archaeologist that officials in Vernon Township, New Jersey, were planning to build soccer and baseball fields on a ten-thousand-year-old Lenape village and burial ground known as Black Creek.

"Our kids need fields," one Vernon Township resident told the *Newark Star-Ledger* newspaper.

Despite an agreement in which the Vernon Civic Association was to study the issue for a month and try to find an alternative or compromise, township work crews began grading the tract, an act seen as a betrayal by the Lenape and their supporters. A Superior Court judge ordered an immediate halt to all work at the site, ruling later that the township was forbidden to disturb the area, pending a review by the New Jersey Historic Preservation Office.

"This is not just some tools Indians once used," Urie "Fox Sparrow" Ridgeway, a Tribal Council member, told a state review board for historic sites. "It is our past, it is our present, and it is our future. This is where our ancestors played, had children, and lived."

The dispute raged on. Eventually, the state sided with the Lenape, designating the tract as "historic." In the early spring of 2005, the entire site was purchased by the state to protect it from development in perpetuity.

The problem at Black Creek is the same one the Lenape

have faced since the Europeans first stepped ashore in America: people want their land. And, increasingly, there's not enough to go around.

Even in Cumberland and Salem Counties, far from New York, there are signs of new development. Marion Strong Medicine is surprised and concerned at the number of new houses that have popped up in Burden's Hill. One is an expensive-looking A-frame, like something you might see in Switzerland or Aspen, Colorado. She wonders who has the money to build such a home, and worries that this area, too, is doomed to be developed into housing for commuters heading to Philadelphia, Wilmington, Atlantic City, or even New York City.

She is greatly cheered, however, that more than eighteen hundred acres of land in the Burden's Hill Forest were recently saved from development, thanks to a partnership between four private and public entities. There are also numerous "Preserved Farmland" signs, which indicate that the state has purchased, from the owner of the farm, the future development rights.

The land alternates between oak forest and rich wetlands. Wild holly bushes grow in abundance. This region, along with Cape May and Sandy Hook on New Jersey's Atlantic coast, are among the best places in the world to see migratory birds.

For some reason, a memory is sparked, one that she has not mentioned before. She remembers her grandmother's death in the 1920s. "Grandmom," as she called her mother's mother, had died of cancer at the home of one of her mother's sisters. As was the custom of the time, the body was laid in a coffin in the living room where people came to pay their respects. Marion Strong Medicine was so small that she could not see in the coffin. Someone got a stool for her to stand on. Spontaneously, she reached in and took her grandmother's hand and held it, refusing to let go. Finally, one of the women gently pulled her hand away and took her to another room. Her "other" grandmother—her father's mother—arrived and took her home with her.

Marion Strong Medicine was already learning that women were in charge of the most important moments of family life, including death. In the Lenape culture, women were—and are—powerful figures. In fact, their input on key decisions for the tribe, as well as within their own families, is an ancient tradition.

16

Well, this is the way it works. If you're going to get something done in our tribe, you just get the women together and we'll tell the men what to do. Because that is the way the Indian way was. Or at least, the Lenape way.

Traditionally, Indian women sat back and didn't have too much to say to the outside world. White people thought Indian women were shy. Ha!

In my tribe, the women, I would dare say, are basically the brains. Basically the brains, but we let the men think they're the brains. The men were the warriors, but when it came time to go to war, they went inside and consulted the wives first. And if the wives said it was wrong for them to go to war, the women were smart enough to tell them, "Hey, you got to go this way, not that way." So the big chiefs, when they got done talking to their wives, and the wives had their say, then they would go out and tell the warriors whether or not they could go to war.

Listen, men do foolish stuff. I don't know why. Don't ask me to explain it. It's beyond me. When I was a little girl, when the stock market crashed in 1929, you didn't hear about women jumping out the windows. It was the men who were stupid enough to jump out the windows.

"STRONG MEDICINE" SPEAKS

When men live alone, or in groups without women, all kinds of bad stuff happens. That's the truth. Men need women.

It's not that women don't need men. Life would be awfully dull without them. I like having them around. Most of the time. Listen, even the good ones are a pain in the butt sometimes.

Lenape marriage, going way back, is supposed to be a partnership. It's between the two of you, and together you make decisions. You're both thinking the same way after a while, hopefully. And if he wants to be the wheel, let him be the wheel. You don't care if you're the hubcap or something. As long as you're both compatible. If you can see his side, and he can see your side, that's what matters. As long as you can talk about it, decide what you're going to do about it, and do it, what difference does it make if he has the idea—wrong though it may be—that he's in charge?

If you look back at history, you see that women have always been strong. Stronger than people give them credit for. Look at these white women who came to America, the ones that went out west in covered wagons. Look how much those women did. I think the majority of women, from way back when, weren't hopelessly helpless. They were made out to be second-class citizens, but really and truly I bet many weren't. They did have power, but they had to be careful how they used it. If they didn't let a man be the wheel, a white woman might be reprimanded or destroyed.

It's still true today for a lot of women throughout the world. They're treated like property. Like they're nothing. I'm very glad I'm Lenape. And I'm glad I was born in the United States of America, where women have more options and more control of their lives than in many places.

I believe a woman can be feminine and still be strong. I don't think the two things contradict each other. Just look at me—yes, I'm very feisty but, oh, I love fashion and all that kind of stuff. I always made all of my own clothes, and when I had any extra money, I'd buy myself a really fine piece of material and make a new dress or coat. I love to wear hats, and I love to have a new hairstyle.

In fact, with my hair, I was always a little vain. Back in the forties I used to try and have those big, fancy hairstyles that the movie stars wore. Honey, it was hard work. I had a lot of hair, very thick, and it just didn't want to stay put. When I was a senior in high school I was on the girls' basketball team, and my hair would keep falling down in my eyes. They'd have to stop the game because I couldn't see, and everyone would wait while I'd put pins in my hair and try to nail it back down. Looking back on it now, I have to laugh at myself. I think it's pretty silly.

One time, when the boys were little, I got a really fancy hairdo in Philadelphia. My aunt wanted to take me to a champagne sip, which is a fancy party, and my uncle offered to watch the boys. I think this was when Wilbur was overseas, during the war.

Well, I wanted to look special, so my aunt suggested I go to Gimbels. So I went there and they did up my hair with this huge poof on top, and another poof in back. Well, that was fine, I had this poof, some great big rolls up here, it was beautiful. Oh, boy.

157

But when I went to sleep that night, I must have slept on one side, because when I got up in the morning one of my poofs was smashed flat against the side of my head! They had used so much stiffening stuff that I couldn't fix it, so finally I had to wash it out. Either that, or walk around with a lopsided head all day.

Oh, I love to wear heels—always have. I have moccasins, of course, but when I was coming up, we couldn't wear Indian clothes, and I got used to wearing heels.

I'll tell you a story. One time, back in the 1940s, I used my high-heel shoe to defend myself. In those days we wore these spiked heels, shoes that were real skinny on the bottom.

Anyway, this one time Wilbur and I went to a party. There was a man there who kept bothering me. He was the type of guy who wanted to pinch you all the time, and I don't go for that. I was sitting on the couch, and he sat down next to me, but I noticed he kept inching closer and closer.

I told him, "Hey, you better stay in your place," and what-not. I tried to ignore him but he wouldn't stop, so I said, "If you don't stop bothering me, you're going to get my heel in your head."

Somebody else came in and sat between us but when that person got up and left, here he comes, sliding over again. So I said, "I already told you once, if you don't want my heel in your head, you better leave me alone." Well, he wouldn't take no for an answer, so I took off my shoe and I whacked him in the head with it. I didn't bust his scalp or anything, but he had quite a welt there.

I don't know where Wilbur was during all this—probably

out on the porch or something—but I told him about it later. He said, "Well, Marion, I always knew you could take care of yourself."

A few years later, Wilbur got the idea that I should learn how to use a gun. We were having trouble in the neighborhood with a Peeping Tom, and Wilbur thought I should be able to protect myself and the boys if he wasn't home. The Peeping Tom used to bother one lady in particular, by sneaking up alongside her house and trying to get a look at her while she took her bath in her kitchen on Saturday nights.

Well, one night Wilbur went to a Shriners' meeting. I was home with Mark and Billy. I heard something outside and I went to investigate. Well, there was a man sneaking through the cornfields behind our house. I called out to him and he didn't answer. I had Wilbur's gun with me. It was a German hand-gun—a Luger—that Wilbur took off some dead Nazi and brought home from the war. I called out, "Stop or I'll shoot!" Well, he ran! So I fired the gun, but I missed.

A few weeks later, it was the same scenario. Wilbur wasn't home, it was a Saturday night, and the Peeping Tom was on the prowl. This time, I was upstairs doing something and I heard the boys yelling. They sounded scared, which was unusual, so I run downstairs, and they said, "Mom, there's someone in the out-house!"

My first reaction was anger. Pure rage. Oh, I was nasty-mad. On the warpath! I thought, How dare somebody sneak around here and bother my children? So I told the boys to stay in the house, and I went outside with the gun in my hand, and I yelled, "Hey! I know there's somebody in that outhouse, and

I've got a gun! I'm going to shoot one bullet into the air. If you don't come out, after that, I'm going to empty this gun into the side of that outhouse!"

Well, nothing happened, so I fired that gun into the air. About two seconds later the door flung open so hard I thought the hinges would break, and I saw a man skedaddle into the cornfields. He ran like a bat out of hell, let me tell you.

But I got a look at him, and realized he lived right up the road. I thought, "Well, I'll be darned." Anyway, he never bothered anybody again. Maybe I scared him into behaving. Either that, or he just got old.

I still have that gun. Hope I don't ever need to use it. But I would, if I had to. You never know—the Klan might come back, and I'm going to be ready.

17

Women do a lot of work that nobody really recognizes. And yet, it's really important work, like child care and taking care of Elders. But also, just keeping things moving smoothly.

One of the things I did, over many years, was to help my husband with his business. Almost all of Wilbur's working life, he worked for himself. Mostly he built small houses, put on additions to houses, or did major repairs like putting on a new roof.

I had a hand in it, even when I worked at the sewing factory. I did the books for the construction business when I got home at night. Sometimes I'd be up until two o'clock in the morning, doing estimates and preparing bills, but I still had to go to my own job in the morning.

Wilbur had several men who worked for him regularly, usually four at a time, and they would meet at our house in the morning. While Wilbur was getting dressed, I'd give them coffee and doughnuts, and they'd discuss the plans for the day before heading out to the job site. I learned a lot from them, and from Wilbur, and before long, I was fairly knowledgeable.

Sometimes I would visit the job site if I knew Wilbur hadn't. I would try to surprise the guys to see if they were working hard, doing the job right, and so on. I would try to pull up in my car from a different direction than they expected, or I would park my car out of sight and walk up to the job to see what was really going on. Sometimes I would catch them sitting there, BSing and all this kind of stuff. They would get mad, but I didn't care. It was costing us money to pay them to do nothing.

Wilbur was fine with it for a long time. But then somebody must have said something to him, because one day he asked our son Mark, "Who's the boss here—me or your mom? Who tells the guys what to do?"

Mark told him, "Well, Dad, Mom always knows what's supposed to be done." That wasn't what Wilbur wanted to hear. One thing about Mark, he will tell the truth. That's why he makes such a good Chief.

Well, Wilbur sulked about it for a few days, and after that I tried harder not to overshadow him. I decided to go into the construction business full time and get out of my husband's hair.

I realized I should get a building inspector's license from the state, so I took the classes and passed the test. I was the only woman in the class, but nobody said a word about it. I suppose the instructor might have said, "Hey, what are you doing here?" or found some way to run me off. But he didn't. Not that it would have stopped me, anyway.

I got a job at a public housing project where I had to oversee contractors who came in to do specific jobs. I also had two guys working for me who were supposed to do the regular maintenance, but they were the laziest pair of no-goods I ever saw. I'd have fired them if I'd been able to.

Those two drove me nuts. You give 'em a new smoke alarm, or a light fixture to put up in a bathroom, and you'd go and check it out later, and it wasn't done. They'd say, "Oh, that's not part of my job."

They didn't care, even if it meant someone might get hurt! There was one particular building, two stories high, and every time it rained, the water was running over all the time, right by the doorway. I was afraid someone would slip and fall. I told the guys, "You're going to have to clean those gutters, and I mean now." But as soon as I turned my back, they disappeared again.

Finally I did it myself. I went and got this great big tall ladder and I drug it over to this building and I put it up there. One of the guys said, "Hey, you're going to hurt yourself." I said, "I've got news for you! Somebody's got to check this job out!"

And that's what I did. I cleaned out the leaves and I fixed that guttering.

While I was doing that, though, one of the guys called my boss, who came all the way down there. We didn't see him all the time. He got out of his car and walked over and looked up at me and he said, "Marion, what on earth are you doing? You come on down from there." But I said, "I'm not coming down 'til this job's done." I was really fed up.

The last job I had before I retired was in Atlantic City, about an hour away. Wilbur and I used to take Billy and Mark over there when they were little. The beach was beautiful. You'd walk on the boardwalk and eat ice cream or saltwater taffy. Oh, it was lovely.

Atlantic City was a place where families could spend the

day. Then it began to go downhill. Eventually, in the late seventies, a law was passed and the big wheels were allowed to open gambling casinos there. By the time I was working there, in the 1980s, it was like there were two different Atlantic Cities—the casinos, and the poor part of town.

I worked for the Housing Authority, and some of the things that went on there, in the public housing, was just terrible. Sometimes the tenants would go crazy and just destroy the place. The men would put their foot through a door, or a fist. So I called HUD, at the federal government, and got the money to put up solid-core doors. But when they couldn't put a hole through those doors, they'd go and tear the hinges off! Well, the root of the problem was drugs. Not that everybody was doing drugs, but every family was affected by it in some way.

I had men working for me and they either didn't have a problem working for a woman or they got over it. There was one fellow I got along with particularly well. He was hired as a building inspector, and if he had a question about a roof or some other job, he'd come get me. I'd put on a pair of coveralls, a pair of Oxfords, a hard hat, and gloves, and we'd go to the site.

Now this man, he trusted my judgment. If I wasn't satisfied with what I saw, then he would go back and tell the workers what I'd said, and make 'em do it over again.

I guess my job in Atlantic City was a "man's job," but I never really thought of it that way. Because I grew up as a Lenape woman, I really didn't think there was any job I couldn't do.

PART VIII

Native Pride

JULY 4, 1976, WAS A DAY of great celebration, as Americans marked the two-hundredth anniversary of the signing of the Declaration of Independence. In Bridgeton, New Jersey, patriotic citizens held their share of festivities, with picnics and hot air balloons during the day and fireworks lighting up the night sky.

That same summer in Bridgeton, a small group of people were gathering quietly, hard at work on a different kind of declaration: freedom from fear. Among their short-term decisions was to form a nonprofit agency, "The Nanticoke Lenni-Lenape Indians of New Jersey."

This was the modern reorganization of the tribe. Two years later, on August 7, 1978, five individuals—Mark Gould, Harry S. Jackson, Marion Gould, Carol Gould, and Edith Pierce—signed legal papers incorporating as a nonprofit organization.

It was a proud statement to the world. "It was like we were announcing, 'We are still here,' " Mark Gould recalls three decades later. "There had always been tribal leadership, and the tribe had never ceased to exist, so it wasn't as if we were creating something new. But we were bringing the tribe out into the open. It was like saying, 'We aren't going to live a lie anymore.' "

The attorney who handled the incorporation papers recommended that the tribe follow New Jersey statutes, with written bylaws and nine elected officers. Mark Gould was elected tribal chairman; Harry S. Jackson, assistant tribal chairman; Marion Gould, secretary; Carol Gould, treasurer; and five others, who were at-large members.

On December 7, 1982, another milestone was achieved when the tribe received official recognition from the state of New Jersey. By that time, about 150 people had become dues-paying members of the organization. Today, there are more than 2,800, with another 1,500 individuals who are involved but not enrolled as tribal citizens.

The tribe's revival was part of a great historical movement in the United States, one that is largely unheralded in mainstream America. It is the American Indian civil rights movement in which Native Americans are working, in an organized way, to reestablish tribes as sovereign governments in their own right.

Tied to the tribal sovereignty movement is the cultural reawakening known as "Native Pride." Instead of denying or disparaging their heritage, Indians are encouraged, by their leaders, to celebrate it.

Scholars recognize the significance of the movement, even if many Americans do not. "The Indian revival of the second half of the twentieth century deserves to be recognized as a major episode in American history," writes Charles Wilkinson, a law professor at the University of Colorado, in his book *Blood Struggle: The Rise of Modern Indian Nations*. "The modern tribal sovereignty movement can fairly be mentioned in the same breath with the abolitionists and suffragists of old and the contemporary civil rights, women's, and environmental movements."

In the late 1960s and early 1970s, some Native Americans had begun asserting their rights in ways that created controversy, most notably in February 1973, when the American Indian Movement, known as AIM, took control of South Dakota's Wounded Knee to protest the way that the Pine Ridge Reservation was being governed. The occupation lasted more than two months and resulted in two deaths.

Few Americans, however, seemed to understand the depth of Native Americans' frustration and despair. The quality of life, especially on reservations, was significantly below the general population in terms of poverty, access to jobs, health care, education, and life expectancy.

One of the most contentious issues centered on religious practices. Despite the promise of freedom of religion that is a central part of the U.S. Constitution, the right of Native Americans to freely practice their religions was not fully protected until August 11, 1978, when Congress passed into law the American Indian Religious Freedom Act.

The Lenape had been converted to Christianity hundreds of years earlier by European missionaries but continued to quietly maintain their own belief system. "We are a Christian people," Chief Gould says, "but we are also Lenape, and we do not believe the two conflict with one another."

Russell Bourne, a historian who is a member of the Institute of American Indian Studies, has studied this phenomenon. "Compared to the clashes of religious empires in Europe and Asia (which tended to be matters of wipeout or amalgamation), something quite different occurred in America's northeastern woodlands," Bourne writes in his book *Gods of War, Gods of Peace*. As he explains it, there was "change through interaction" that "dramatically altered but did not blend the peoples' separate cultures, resulting in a strangely uncombined, uniquely American civilization. It resembles that of no other nation on earth."

Unlike some native peoples, the Lenape had always believed in only one god, whom they call "Creator" (literally, "He Who Creates Us by His Thoughts") among other appellations descriptive of the Creator's activity or perceived character, according to the Reverend Dr. John "Smiling Thunderbear" Norwood, who is both a Protestant minister and a Tribal Council member. "The Christian God and the Indian Creator are, to the Lenape, the same," he explains. "For Nanticoke and Lenape converts to Christianity, the Christian Bible brought new revelations about the Creator, in whom the Lenape had always believed."

The essential difference is not in theology but in the way the two religions are practiced—rituals around a fire in a Sacred Circle as opposed to an altar or pulpit. Just as Christians believe in life after death, the Lenape believe that their ancestors have "gone on" to the Spirit World or Sky World, where they will one day join them.

Europeans were perplexed by the Lenape view of the natural world, and how they perceived their place in it.

Heckewelder, an early missionary quoted in Bourne's book, wrote that the Lenape see themselves as a part of nature, "from which they have not yet ventured to separate themselves."

As part of their religious observances, the Lenape express reverence for (but not worship of) the sun and moon, Indian corn, and the four directions: East, which represents the rising sun and the beginning of each new day and new life; North, which brings hardships and discomforts, such as the cold winds of winter; South, which brings the good things of life, including the warmth of summer and the growing season; and West, where the sun sets, marking the end of each day but also of life itself.

At any gathering of the Lenape, it is common to see both Lenape and Christian religious practices. One place where it occurs frequently is musical performance and expression.

On a rainy Saturday evening, for example, nine young men sit cross-legged on the floor, encircling an enormous drum, perhaps six feet across, made from deerskin long ago. Each has a baton, and they beat the drum in perfect unison. On this particular day, they are practicing a new song, written in the language of the Nanticokes.

These young men are just as likely to sing and drum, however, to a Christian hymn. A particular favorite of the tribe is "Will the Circle Be Unbroken," because of its reference to circles, the shape that is incorporated into religious ceremonies because it represents the cycle of the seasons and of life itself. The words were modified for an Indian round dance by John Smiling Thunderbear:

"STRONG MEDICINE" SPEAKS

May the circle be unbroken!
By and by, Lord, by and by.
There's a better home a-waiting
In the sky, Lord, in the sky.
Drums are beating, voices singing
There is joy all round and round.
The Lord has kept us all together
And his love and peace abound.

But perhaps the most poignant example of combined Christian and Lenape religious practices can be seen during death rituals. When Wilbur Gould died, the fact that Marion Strong Medicine was able to openly hold Indian as well as Christian funeral rites for her husband was deeply meaningful. Without the American Indian civil rights movement and "Native Pride," it would not have happened.

18

In the old days, I would not have been able to say good-bye to my husband at the Sacred Circle. I am very grateful that I was able to do that.

We had three services for Wilbur. The one held at the Sacred Circle was first. The second was a Christian funeral and burial in the Methodist churchyard. And, after that, some of our fellow Lenape out in Oklahoma, on the reservation, honored him in a service where they raised up his name.

My husband was raised Methodist, but I have been a Seventh-day Adventist my whole life, like my mom and my aunts. When white people first came four hundred years ago, they brought their religion with them, and they converted us.

But even though we became Christians, we continued our Indian customs. When a Lenape hunter kills an animal, he leaves a small amount of tobacco at the site to thank the Creator for the gift. When Lenape people cut down a tree—which they try never, ever to do—we pray to the Creator, apologizing to Him.

The Methodist Church that we call "the Indian church" has an interesting history. The Methodists came and built it, but then they pretty much left us alone there. During the years we were a hidden people, it's one of the few places where we could meet safely. It's still the home church for many members of the tribe. To this day, when there is a fifth Sunday in a month, they hold an Indian service there.

Our tribe also has a longtime relationship with Quakers. If you look back at history, the Quakers tried to defend the rights of the Lenape. In fact, we have a relationship with them that continues to this day. The Philadelphia Friends send a donation every year to help us with our Powwow. I don't know how that got started, or how long it's been going on, but it's a nice gesture. They want us to thrive.

The Lenape have always believed in one God, the Creator, so I guess it was easy for us to accept Christianity in our lives when we first heard about it. We felt the Christian God and our Creator must be one and the same.

According to the religious history of the Lenape, called the Wallum Olum, our people migrated to the North American continent across the Bering Strait. We believe our ancestors migrated across the continent, crossed the Mississippi River, and eventually made their way to what is now called New York, New Jersey, and Pennsylvania. Legend has it that there were no human beings living here, which is why we came to be called the "Original People" or the "Grandfather People."

I am talking about ten thousand years ago, maybe more. No one knows for sure. Some white scholars cast doubt on the Wallum Olum, or at least the version of it that was written down by one white guy a century ago. I don't see what gives these white people the right to be quibbling about it. It's our story, not theirs.

If they want to help us by studying and researching it, that's one thing. They are welcome to do that. But they should work with us, and listen to what we have to say.

Part of being an American is practicing your religion as you see fit. That's fundamental. It's a basic right. But the Europeans wanted to squelch our religions from day one. By trying to stop us from practicing our religions, they were basically trying to get rid of us.

The Indian civil rights movement, and what we call Native Pride, is something that had to come from within ourselves. There's only so long people can be told they're second-class citizens, that they're no good. They're either going to self-destruct or find a way to make a stand.

When the time came that our tribe—all the tribes—began to assert themselves, and to be proud again, I think some of the older generation was worried. Some of them are still worried— they want things to stay the same. A little afraid to rock the boat. But not me! I was all for it. One hundred percent. I am proud that I signed the incorporation papers back in '78, and that I served as one of the first trustees.

Part of Native Pride is teaching the children who they are, and that our culture has value. We have to teach them to reject the image of Indians that was invented in Hollywood. People get their idea of what Indians are like from books and movies, especially those "Westerns" where the cowboys are the good guys and the Indians are the bad guys. Well, they need to get with the times. That's not the way it is—and it never was. That was Hollywood talking.

I don't see how they can call us the "bad" guys when all we were doing was protecting our families, our land, our way of life. You'd do the same thing if someone invaded your property and tried to take it from you.

There used to be this saying that you'd hear in the movies: "The only good Indian is a dead Indian." Well, how crazy is that? And they still play those movies on TV. You can see them any time of day or night.

I don't think a lot of non-Natives are aware of what happened to the Indians. When I was coming up, they never even mentioned it in school. I think they do today, but it's sort of glossed over quickly. It's still from the white point of view.

When I was coming up, I don't remember a single movie about Indians that was accurate. In fact, the only movie I could relate to had nothing to do with Indians. It was the movie The Grapes of Wrath, based on the book by John Steinbeck. I could sympathize with those poor Okies losing their land and their homes during the Depression. The grandpa didn't want to leave. They took him along because they couldn't leave him behind, and he died on the road to California. When I read that book in high school and saw the movie, I thought, "That's just what has happened to the Indian people!"

Recently I read about an Indian woman who was trying to get the government to compensate Indians, because she felt that the United States owed the Indians something. But I don't think that will ever happen. How can they pay us back? They'd have to turn over the whole country to us.

Now you have some tribes that have figured out how to make money by operating casinos. That worries me, because it doesn't have anything to do with traditional values. But a lot of

Indian people are desperate. A lot of them are very, very poor and their leaders are looking for a quick fix, anything that will bring some money into the community.

In our tribe, we are not interested in pursuing gambling. In fact, our Tribal Council passed a resolution against it. We are working on creating other types of economic opportunities to help our people get jobs, education, and training. We think we'll be better off in the long run.

The tribes that are involved in gambling, I wonder if the big wheels are still keeping 'em down. I wonder how much of the money really gets to the Indian people who need it the most. And then you get these white people claiming they have Indian blood just so they can get some of that casino money! If that isn't the most doggone thing I ever heard.

Whenever there's money to be made, it seems to me that the "little guy" gets hurt. There was a piece in the paper a couple of years ago which I still remember. It was about this little old Indian lady out west. She didn't have a decent house, but somebody was getting oil right from her yard! They were giving her a pittance compared to what the oil was worth. And she had hardly anything to eat. Now, that's a sin and a shame, if you ask me. It's the same old thing—"Hey, get out of the way. We want what you got."

These attitudes are not an easy thing to combat, but we, as a people, are certainly working on it. The first hurdle is refusing to accept how someone else defines you. When you've heard that you're nothing for a long, long time, and you don't deserve to have rights, then after a while you start to believe it. And it becomes part of who you are.

So that's what the Native Pride movement did, and is still doing. It's saying, "We are human beings, too. We deserve to be treated with respect."

Only recently have Indians really had a chance to be themselves as a people. Most people don't know it, but Indians were not citizens until 1924. That's pretty late in the game, if you ask me!

Bitterness won't help us one bit, though, and I think most Indians recognize this. You can't move forward, tackle the challenges in life, enjoy the good things, if you're so mad you can't see straight. As long as you dwell on it, then I think you're no better than the other guy.

19

Indian people are still lagging behind the rest of America in many ways—poverty, health care, education. Generally, the ones who seem to suffer the most are the tribes living on government reservations.

You can't just shove people off somewhere like they're animals in a zoo, but that is what white people have tried to do to Indians who were put on reservations. When you don't have control over your life, and the future looks hopeless, that is a very difficult way to live. What has been done to Indians—the mass killings, the treaties that were lies, being pushed off our land, being sent to reservations—is the biggest crime in American history, except for slavery, which is right up there with it.

I am very grateful that I never had to live on a reservation. I am certain the people of my tribe are much better off. It's awful hard to find a job, or get an education, if you're stuck on a reservation. You don't have as many choices. And a lot of the tribes are far from their original homelands, which must be very painful for them.

What the government would do is send people from Washington to tell the Indians what to do and how to live. Of course, the people sent by the government would be white. Nobody bothered to consider that Indians are human beings, with our own culture. I believe the Indian people would be okay now if, way back when, the government had just left us alone.

I have visited several reservations. I have not been to the ones where the Lenape live, not yet, anyway. I'm not sure how I would feel about that.

In the 1970s, Wilbur and I went west on several road trips. The first time, we went to St. Louis to visit his old army friend, and from there we went all the way to San Francisco, stopping at a reservation in the Dakotas on the way. And we were just amazed, just appalled, because it seemed like they had these Indians all caged in.

When we pulled on the property, we didn't see anybody, except maybe a dog. There's nobody outside. Wilbur and I wanted to meet some people, see if we had anything in common, just say hello, but we didn't get much of a chance.

Well, we drove down this dirt road and I saw a man outside a trailer, so we stopped and I got out and greeted him. First thing you know, he sends his dog after me. The dog was growling and circling me, and I said to the man, "Hey, I'm Indian, all I want to do is say hi, please call off your dog." But he wouldn't do it. So I said, "Mister, I have a gun and if I have to use it, I will. Now, call off your dog." So he did. But then he went back in the trailer. Wilbur wanted to keep driving along the dirt road and see if we could meet someone friendlier but I said, "No, I think we better get out of this place."

Another time when we went out west, we stopped at a reservation in Arizona. It was the first of the month. They'd gotten some money in the mail—government checks, I guess—and they drank it all up. And you never saw so many drunken Indians in your life. I mean, they were laying down all over the place! I have never seen any drinking like that in my life.

Sure, there are people in our tribe who drink too much. But I don't think it's any more of a problem than in the general population. So I think drinking and living on a reservation go hand in hand.

It's easy to judge, but you have to have some compassion. You have to ask yourself, "How did they get this way?" It's just like in the housing projects where I worked in Atlantic City. These are forgotten people. Some of them are good folks, just down on their luck. Maybe being a black person living in a housing project in Atlantic City is just like being Indian on a reservation—you're stuck there and nobody cares.

I think Indians have more say in how reservations are run today. I know that has been improving. Some of the Indians have come up in the world, they've gone to college, some are lawyers. But there's still that little thing that says, "You can go so far, but we're not going to let you go any further." I'd love to be in that kind of position where I could fight the people holding us back because I'd enjoy myself.

If you want to know what it feels like to have your land stolen from you, talk to these people who are upset about this thing they call "eminent domain." That's when the government can come along and take your home and tear it down so they can build a road or a school. Well, nowadays, they take people's land and give it to some rich developer to build a high-rise on it. That is wrong! But that's what has been done to the Indians for the past four hundred years: "We want your land, now get out of the way."

I don't hate the government. It's just that I don't trust it. The federal government is responsible for what they have done to the Indians. I don't think you can be Indian and feel all warm and fuzzy about the federal government, unless you have amnesia.

It's sad to say, but I think most Americans forget Indians were here first. They say, "America is a nation of immigrants." You hear that all the time. But I'm not an immigrant! No one who is Native American is an immigrant. All I can say is, "Please remember that. Be decent to us. Be fair. Try to understand. We are Americans, too."

I've been a good citizen all my life. I pay my taxes, and I vote in elections. I almost lost my husband in World War II. On Memorial Day, I've got my American flag flying outside my porch, just like everybody else. I'm proud to be an American. But I'm proud to be Indian, too.

This is the way I see it: We've been here for ten thousand years. The United States government has been here for less than two hundred and fifty. I don't think the government has the right to tell Indian people what to do, where to live, or to put us in a corner somewhere.

PART IX

Full Circle

MARION STRONG MEDICINE arrives at the tribe's twenty-fifth annual Powwow with her sister-in-law Margaret Gould Pierce, and the two women immediately make the rounds, saying hello to old friends and new acquaintances.

By coincidence, both are wearing bright pink blouses. Strong Medicine also sports a large-brimmed straw hat. As they walk, they munch happily on frybread—fried dough with powdered sugar and jam or honey, an Indian favorite. There is powdered sugar on Strong Medicine's nose. "I would hug you," she says, laughing, when she greets a friend, "but I don't want to get powdered sugar all over you."

Unlike spiritual gatherings, which are held on the tribe's private property in Cumberland County, the Powwow is held at a county fairgrounds in nearby Salem County, and is open to the public. A significant proportion of those in attendance—perhaps one third or more—are white or African American. Many have come from Philadelphia, just across the Delaware River, for the day. Echoing a national trend, their presence is evidence of growing interest in Native American culture among non-Natives. The Smithsonian's National Museum of the American Indian, which opened on the Mall in Washington, D.C., the previous September, has reported record-breaking attendance.

The Powwow is also attended by members of many other tribes from across the nation. Some are vendors, selling native food and crafts. Others are here to compete in dance competitions that are a highlighted part of the two-day event.

The Chief speaks to the crowd, explaining that no one should enter the circle where the dancers will be performing. He adds that if an eagle feather falls to the ground during a dance, only a member of the tribe who has been

Lia "Watching Sparrow" Gould, youngest
of the Chief's three daughters, in 2005.

trained to carry out religious duties may pick it up. While all birds are considered special creatures to the Lenape, he explains, the eagle is especially cherished because it soars the highest and thus is nearest to the Creator and ancestors who have entered the Spirit World.

One of the highlights is the traditional dance by the Lenape women. This is Marion Strong Medicine's favorite part. Her granddaughter Lia Watching Sparrow won the contest to be this year's Indian Princess and is among the featured dancers. Tribal Council member Urie "Fox Sparrow" Ridgeway leads the Red Blanket Singers, whose haunting melodies in the ancient language are punctuated with drumbeats that make the ground tremble.

The Powwow represents a yearlong effort on the part of many volunteers, led by Gail Gentle Leaves, the Chief's wife. In good years, if the weather holds, a small profit is made by the tribe, but the main reason the Powwow is held is to share their culture with others in a neighborly way.

To Elders such as Marion Strong Medicine, the fact that the tribe can now be so open about its heritage is a source of great joy.

Chief Mark "Quiet Hawk" Gould
at the tribe's Powwow in 2006.

20

In some ways, it's the Powwow that seems the most amazing to me. I never thought I'd see the day that my great-grandchildren would be able to wear Indian clothes in public, to dance traditional dances, and "drum" at the county fairgrounds, for heaven's sake. It is very interesting to see all these people come and watch and treat us respectfully. Remember, I came up in the days of the KKK.

The other thing that I think is just grand is that we bought our own piece of property for our private gatherings. It's a place where we can retreat from the outside world.

We laid the groundwork for this in my generation, and the kids—my kids' generation—ran with it. Now the next generation is beginning to do their part.

I really do feel that I have been a witness to history. My biggest contribution is Mark! My husband and I brought Mark into this world, and apparently we did a pretty good job. Heck, we put up with him all those years. Who knew he would have leadership abilities?

Of course, I am proud of my other two sons, too. It was their choice not to be involved in the tribe to the same degree that

Mark is. I have no problem with that. Each child is different and reaches out for different things.

It took a long time for the tribe to raise the money we needed to buy our land. Everything we've done, it's been one step at a time. We raised money in bake sales and by "passing the hat" at tribal gatherings. Mary "Spreading Eagle Wings" Ward, one of my high school classmates, was a genius at fund-raising. She is ill now; she's had several strokes. But she was a go-getter, always coming up with these clever ideas. For

Chief Mark "Quiet Hawk" Gould in
traditional dress with his eldest grandchild,
Steffani Savoy, at the tribe's Powwow,
held at the Salem County, New Jersey,
Fairgrounds, circa 1991.

A Lenni-Lenape boy awaits his turn
to dance at the tribe's 2005 Powwow.

instance, she put together these little bags of soil and mailed them to all of the families in the tribe with a fund-raising pitch saying, "This is your land!" It worked. All the families sent in what they could.

This was in the 1970s and 1980s. I was still working full time, but I was very, very happy that things were moving forward for the tribe. In my free time, though, I did make albums of photographs, memorabilia, and local newspaper clippings about the tribe's activities. I wanted to create a historical record.

Now, I know a thing or two about the land around here, but when they started looking at land I kept quiet, for once in my life. I tend to take over sometimes, and I didn't want to undermine my son! Part of the Indian way is the belief that the older

Women dancers in traditional clothing perform a formal dance at a recent Powwow. The woman in the center, with arm extended, is Tina "Little Wild Flower" Pierce Fragoso, an anthropologist and member of the Tribal Council.

generation should know when to step aside. It's true that Elders are treated with respect, and the younger folks do listen when we have something to say.

But if the older generation doesn't know when to step back, the younger generation never learns how or when to step up to the plate. It was obvious to me that Mark and the others knew what they were doing. And since they were the ones who were going to be responsible, it only seemed fair to keep out of it.

If you want your young people to be a part of the tribe, you have to involve them, encourage them, and then let them go. I don't think the older generation should say, "It's got to be like this, because this is the way we want it." No, that's not the way it should be. It should be continual. You're in charge, then they're in charge. It should be in such a way that everybody feels like part of the tribe.

So one day I heard that Mark and the others were very close to buying a specific piece of land. They had already looked at several places and I had gone on my own to check them out.

When Mark told me they'd made the decision and bought twenty-eight acres over in Fairfield Township, I was pleased because I think it is an excellent piece of land. But more than that, I felt very emotional. It was a long time coming. To think that our people had our own piece of land! And no one was going to take it away from us!

After we bought it, I drove over there by myself, parked my

A member of the tribe, Denise "Bright Dove" Dunkley,
completes the circle at the 2005 annual Powwow.

car, and walked around. Just getting there is a beautiful drive. It's all countryside, nothing but farms. The road's not even marked. You have to know where it is. There's an old stone church, with a very old graveyard and an iron fence. You turn behind there and drive a couple of miles. I just listened to the birds and the other sounds of Mother Earth. If you stand still long enough, and use all your senses, you become part of it.

The tribe started holding spiritual gatherings there, especially in spring and fall, and that's where we keep our Sacred Circle. Last year we put up our first building on the site, a pole barn. Eventually we hope to construct a building there shaped like a turtle, which is the symbol of our tribe.

Lenape people believe that the origin of the earth stems from a turtle's back. Everything was covered with water until a tree started growing on the back of a big turtle, and the turtle allowed the first people to take shelter there or they'd have drowned. So we've always had great fondness for turtles and tortoises. One time, when Wilbur and I were traveling out west, we stopped at a nature preserve where they had an enormous tortoise. The people there let me ride on its back! That was a strange experience. Boy, did I get a kick out of it. And it didn't seem to bother the tortoise one bit.

The building shaped like a turtle is a longtime dream of the tribe's. Some years back, my granddaughter Ty and I made some drawings, just for fun, of what it might look like. Later, they had an architect draw up the plans formally. They are beautiful!

We want to have room for meetings and a place to keep our archives for future generations. We see it as a place for education for the children, not just our children but anyone who wants to come and see who we are, as long as they are respectful.

Most of the land, of course, will be kept natural out of respect to Mother Nature. There are open fields—part of it was probably farmed at one time—but also some marshland and woods.

Our property is a place of peace and replenishment. It is not open to the public—that's what the Powwow, held at the Salem County Fairgrounds, is for. Members of the tribe go to our property any time they want, to be alone. The gatherings there are so joyful, it is hard to explain. It is a place to relax, not to be judged by the outside world. I remember Mark coming up to me at one of the first gatherings there. He was so happy that we had a piece of land at last. He said, "So, Mom, what do you think?"

For once in my life I couldn't say a word. I was so proud of my son, and wishing my mother and my aunts, and old grandpop Pierce and the rest of them had lived to see this day. It gives me a grand feeling, knowing my younger people are bringing back the old ways.

I have been a witness to history. We are hidden no longer. We are alive and kicking, and we aren't going anywhere!

We have come full circle in my lifetime. I've lived to see a complete turnaround, not just in my tribe, but all American Indians. We don't hate ourselves anymore. And no one's going to take that away from us.

21

Now I will tell you the story of my Indian name: Strong Medicine.

It's all Mark's fault!

First let me explain that being given an Indian name is a very important moment in your life. It is a commitment to living the Indian way for the rest of your life. This is not something that is done lightly. The person who gives it to you must know you well, and they think about it long and hard, sometimes for years.

Once it is given to you, you're stuck with it, whether you like it or not. It's for life. The naming ceremony is one of our most important ceremonies. It is a religious ceremony that is overseen by a person trained as a spiritual leader and is conducted at the Sacred Circle as part of the spring or fall spiritual gathering. Sometimes it is given to children, but often they wait until you're an adult and they can pick something that really fits you.

Sometimes people don't get an Indian name until very late in life. We had one man who got his when he was ninety-two years old. He hadn't been active in the tribe when he was younger. The name chosen for him was Iron Eagle.

Full Circle

I was given my Indian name when I was in my fifties, about twenty-five years ago. This was before the tribe had raised the money to buy our land, so the ceremony was held in the back-yard of one of the Tribal Council members.

Mark stopped by a few days ahead of the gathering and said, "Mom, I've picked out a name for you." And he told me what time to come, where to be, but nothing else. They don't tell you ahead of time. No one consults you about your name.

Wilbur was given his name the same day. Mark picked it out for him. It was "Wise Fox," and I remember thinking, "That's very nice. Very good. Fits him well."

Then came my turn. The spiritual leader asked Mark, who was already the Chief in those days, "What name have you chosen for her, and why?"

Mark said, "She is my mother, and she is knowledgeable about traditional plants and herbs. She is also a person who tells the truth, a person people seek out for honest advice, so the name I have chosen for her is 'Strong Medicine.'"

I almost fell on the ground.

After the ceremony, I said to Mark, "What kind of name is that? That's not a very pretty name to give somebody. I'm not so sure I like it!"

And he said, "But, Mom! It's you!"

Well, I have to admit, I have a strong personality. But still, the name came as something of a surprise. I thought I was going to get something feminine, like "Darting Butterfly" or some-thing like that. Everyone knew I loved butterflies. Gee.

Heck, you never know what people really think of you. But as the years have gone by, I realize my son was right. It suits me well, and since that's the point of an Indian name, I have to admit he chose well.

For example, I gave some advice one time to a man who had abandoned his first wife and children and started another family. After that, he just ignored his children from his first marriage! Well, I happened to run into him when he was old and dying. He was complaining and fretting about this and that—just nonsense—and I said, "Frankly, I can't believe that's what you're worrying about." And he said, "Why, what do you mean?" And I said, "You know you're dying. You said so yourself. You need to reach out to your children from your first marriage and apologize to them before it's too late." So I gave him a little dose of Strong Medicine!

Many people still call me Marion because that's the name they've known me by. For instance, my sister-in-law Margaret has known me for almost seventy years and it wouldn't occur to her to call me anything but Marion.

But Strong Medicine is my official Indian name, and the one that will carry me into the next world.

22

Things were going well for the tribe. Wilbur and I were retired and enjoying life. And then we found out our son Jeff was sick. Very sick.

You never think you're going to outlive one of your children. But that is what happened.

Jeff was the youngest of our three sons. He was a character, just like the other two. He was very smart; he could do almost

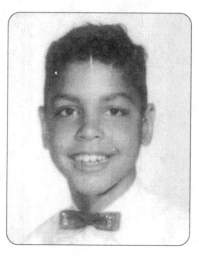

Jeff Gould's school picture, circa 1962.

anything that needed to be done. He could fix any car, anything like that, and he knew how to run all the heavy equipment. He was just something.

And he loved animals. When he was maybe three years old, he found a stray cat in the yard and he decided that it was "his" cat. Oh, how he loved that cat. He'd walk all around with that cat hanging off his arm, hanging down so low its head was practically dragging on the floor. But somehow, the cat never seemed to mind.

Jeff Gould at age three with his kitten, circa 1956.
Jeff was the youngest of the three Gould sons.

As he got older, he was the kind of person who never wasted a minute. He had a friend who had a bus company, and he went to work for him part time, and while the other bus drivers were goofing off during their break, Jeff would read. He had a large curiosity. He had to find out what made everything tick. He would read books on how to do certain things, like how to run a business.

Even as a little boy, Jeff was one of those kind that had to check things out, make sure he knew exactly what was right. And if he wasn't satisfied with somebody's explanation, he had to investigate it himself. If he had to go get a book at the library, he would do so, to get the information he needed.

Jeff never married and he loved to travel anyplace, anytime. He was a free spirit. I bought a camper when I was working for the Atlantic City Housing Authority. When I left the job, Jeff decided that he wanted to go to Florida. He wanted to know if he could take the camper and I said yes.

So off he went.

But then he got sick, and he was going to doctors all the time. He'd call us on the phone, tell us what was going on. Wilbur and I were very upset, and we drove to Florida over and over again to see him. The doctors said he was terminally ill, but I didn't need them to tell me that. I could see it in Jeff's face, in his eyes. There was nothing Wilbur and I could do except be good to him. Finally, I said, "I want you to come home."

It is very difficult for me to talk about him—but one memory I will share was on the trip when we brought him home, he was very tired and we needed to stop and find a hotel for the night. And every hotel seemed to be full. There was one hotel left, and I went to the front desk even though the sign said "No vacancy." I explained that my son was ill and that we were bringing him home for the last time, and wasn't there anything they could do? And, it was a miracle. Just a miracle. Because the man was a good soul, and he said, "I'll help you." And he said there was one room left for emergencies and that we could have it.

We had Jeff's dogs with us, too. Sometimes when I think about those days, I remember him climbing down out of the camper because he insisted on walking those dogs himself. And I can still see him, barely able to stand up, walking his dogs.

Once we got home, it wasn't long before he passed. We all did what we could to make him comfortable. It was Fourth of July and our son Billy likes to have a barbecue at his house next door. It's something we do every year, but Jeff was so weak he couldn't go. You know what Billy did? He did the whole barbecue all over again when Jeff was feeling a little better. He did that for Jeff. He did that for his brother.

Oh, I shouldn't talk about him. It makes my mind all cloudy. I thought it was hard to bury my parents and my brother. But, oh, to bury a son is a terrible thing. He was forty-two years old.

Some years back I had bought a plot in the graveyard over in Gouldtown, next to the church my husband's family had always gone to. I never thought Jeff would be the first one buried there.

Full Circle

But this is life! It's part of living. You can't control things. You have to accept what happens. The Creator, the Lord, does many things we do not understand. Our job is to pick up and keep on going, moving forward, even when there are times when you feel you can't.

PART X

Modern Life

A MILE FROM MARION Strong Medicine's bungalow, past an intersection with a gas station and convenience stores, an enormous water tower signals one's arrival in Bridgeton. Painted long ago on the side, in gigantic scale, is the Bridgeton City insignia, a Lenape Indian.

It is a rare, if strangely offhanded acknowledgment of the past. Like most American cities, Bridgeton dates its official beginnings to the arrival of the first white person, in this case, a settler named Richard Hancock, who arrived in 1686, attracted to the rich terrain and, running through it, a small river—the Cohansey, which empties into the great Delaware Bay. During the following three centuries, the fledgling city evolved and reinvented itself, accommodating waves of immigrants, including Germans, Irish, Italians, and more recently, Mexicans. People of African descent have been a presence since Colonial days, when slavery was legal in New Jersey.

With its tree-lined streets, parks, and even a zoo, Bridgeton is a classic small American city. Economically, it has seen better days, and city leaders are scrambling to find secure footing for its future.

Along one of the city's main streets is a long, narrow storefront building, tucked in among law offices, small restaurants, and shops. A sign on the door reads, "Nanticoke Lenni-Lenape Indians."

This is tribal headquarters. Called simply "the Center" by tribal members, the two-story building is more than a century old, and shows its age through creaking floorboards and cracked plaster. Toward the front there is a small store called Turtle Trading Post. In the back are desks, filing cabinets, and a meeting area. The walls are adorned with framed photographs of Elders in traditional dress, among them the Chief's mother, Marion Strong Medicine.

On a typical day, members of the tribe come and go, stopping by to socialize or, perhaps, to attend a committee meeting on their way home from work. Members of the tribe are carpenters and farmers, teachers and nurses. A generation ago, few were college educated but the number is growing. For example, the eldest son of Smiling Thunderbear and his wife, Tanya Smiling Spiritdove, is a recent graduate of West Point.

For months, members of the tribe have been focused on helping to prepare the application for federal "recognition," an official status that would be advantageous to the tribe, allowing it, for example, to be eligible for certain federal grants. The tribe was officially recognized at the state level in 1982, when the state legislature passed a special resolution. Gaining federal recognition, however, requires an additional, formal effort, with tribal leaders working alongside Elders and genealogists to reconstruct the past.

Their having lived as a hidden people for more than a century makes the process more difficult. The tribe's cousins, the Delaware Indians living on a reservation in Oklahoma, already have federal recognition, but leaders of the New Jersey tribe are in the odd position of having to prove the identity of their people to the same entity—the federal government—that forced them to live as a hidden people in the first place. The irony is not lost on tribal leaders, but true to their long-standing reputation, they are a practical people. They move forward, regardless.

Whether or not they will be awarded federal recognition is a question mark. Compared to some of the larger tribes in the western and Plains states—whose lands were invaded much later—the struggling, East Coast Lenape are lagging in numbers, funds, and power.

There is also the issue of gambling. Federal recognition could, theoretically, open the doors to legal casinos run by the tribe. Although tribal leaders have said they are not interested in pursuing casino gambling, the issue makes some non-Natives uneasy—especially those who have a vested interest in Atlantic City, where gambling has been legal since 1978, and where any nearby competition would be seen as a threat.

Tribal leaders, however, have long been eager to distance themselves from gambling. In fact, the Tribal Council passed an antigambling resolution in 2006, choosing instead to pursue nongambling economic opportunities for the tribe, such as the construction trades, through Turtle Associates, a newly launched tribal corporation.

Economic opportunities aside, it is clear that the tribe's first concern is preservation of its culture. There is great emphasis on teaching the young people traditional skills, including beadwork, drumming, songs, and dances.

The tribe almost lost its native language during the years its members were hidden, and some of the traditional dances and ceremonies were gradually forgotten. Fortunately, some of their Lenape cousins living on the Oklahoma reservation never stopped using the language, and another large band of Lenape, who live in Ontario, Canada, had continued the traditional dances and ceremonies.

In recent years, there has been a concerted effort among the three groups to collaborate and share their knowledge with one another. At a recent spiritual gathering of the New Jersey tribe, for example, an invited guest from Oklahoma gave a language lesson that was attended by young and old.

"In Oklahoma, they are the keepers of the language," Chief Gould says. "In Ontario, they are the keepers of the dances and ceremonies. In New Jersey, we are the keepers of the land. That is what we have to contribute."

The land is the most important of all. "Our people can relearn the language and the dances, but once the land is gone, it's gone," Chief Gould explains. "And there is nothing more important to an Indian than the Ancestral Land."

Preserving the culture, however, takes a backseat to more mundane concerns from time to time. An electrical storm has damaged the center's computers, installed, thanks to a grant, just days earlier. A food program for Elders needs more volunteers. A hole in the ceiling needs repairs by a volunteer carpenter, and until he has time to do it, no one can go upstairs.

On the third Saturday of each month, the center is especially busy. A general tribal meeting—open to all members of the tribe and a few invited guests—is held that evening.

It is often "standing room only." Chief Mark "Quiet Hawk" Gould runs these meetings with a firm hand, in a style that might best be described as no-nonsense. When asked to describe his role as Chief, he says simply, "My job is to get the job done. Period."

To watch him closely over a period of many months, one learns to appreciate the complexity of his leadership skills. He nudges, placates, and smooths the waters. Sometimes he scolds. When truly vexed, he produces a scowl that would have made Custer run and hide. He periodically interrupts himself to make jokes, usually the self-deprecating kind, which the Lenape adore. In his younger days, he was known for a wild streak, and he still makes fun of his misspent youth—motorcycles, fistfights, and alcohol. There are also lots of jokes about strong Lenape women and how he "doesn't stand a chance" if something he wants to do for the tribe is opposed by them.

The Chief's day job as a construction manager for the county is physically demanding of a man of sixty-four years. Like his mother, however, he is a person who hates to be idle. "I am only happy when I am busy," he declares.

A typical tribal meeting is long and intense. There is much work to do, and many decisions to be made. At a recent meeting, representatives of various committees—

Chief Mark "Quiet Hawk" Gould
outside the Smithsonian's National Museum
of the American Indian, April 2005.

Powwow, Turtle Associates, and many others—stand and give their reports. Last but not least is the youth leader, a pretty, teenage girl named Trinity Happy Dancing Feather, the daughter of Smiling Thunderbear and his wife, Smiling Spiritdove. She doesn't look entirely comfortable when it's her turn to speak. Looking down at her notes, she begins to speak softly.

"Whoa, wait a minute," Chief Gould, sitting a few feet away, interrupts. "Stand up straight and speak clearly so people in the back can hear you," he says. Like his mother, the Chief will deliver a dose of strong medicine when necessary, especially when dealing with youth.

She starts again, and, once again, the Chief interrupts. "Wait. What's your name?"

The girl looks at him in amazement. "You know what my name is!" she says with incredulity. "Everyone in this room knows who I am!"

"You don't know that for certain. There may be someone here who hasn't been to a meeting in a while. You should always state your name as part of giving a report."

The girl giggles.

"And none of that," says the Chief, sternly but good-naturedly. As the father of three daughters, now grown, he knows a thing or two about giggling. "None of that 'Hee, hee, hee' stuff," he teases her. "We didn't come here tonight to hear 'Hee, hee, hee' from you. We want to know what your committee is doing, and what you think. You are an important part of the tribe—the most important. You are our future."

The girl waits for the end of the Chief's impromptu lecture, which is meant not just for her but as a reminder to everyone present, young and old. She clears her throat while the audience waits patiently. Finally, she gives her report about youth activities, focusing on a program in which teenagers mentor younger children known as Little Acorns. She receives the loudest applause of the evening when she finishes.

Perhaps she doesn't yet realize how different her life is from that of her Elders—and how much hope for the future is invested in her.

23

There is still a lot of work to be done. I am old and I won't live to see it all, but I hope the young folks keep it going.

Our young people have some pretty big jobs left to tackle. For instance, I would like to see us remembered or acknowledged properly in New York City. Philadelphia has done a better job than New York, going all the way back to William Penn in the 1600s, who acted honorably toward us. But New York City has really failed us.

In New York City, I have heard there are only two statues of Lenape Indians, and both of them show a Lenape man "selling" Manhattan to the Dutch—the biggest swindle of all time. I think it's way past time they took those statues down.

Yes, the attitude toward Indians has improved during my lifetime. But it hasn't been fixed entirely, either. People probably walk past those statues in New York City every day on their way to work and think nothing of it. Do they wonder what happened to the Lenape? Do they care?

Sometimes, it almost feels like the world has moved on, without even pausing to think about us. Especially since the terrorist attack, September 11, and America has all these new sets of problems. People of color are still lagging behind but it's not the main issue. I read in the newspaper that supposedly, things are so much better for black people than they used to be. Well, it seems to me that black people are still on the bottom of the heap as far as education, housing—all the important stuff. Indians are on the bottom, too, only sometimes I think people have forgotten us altogether.

The fact that we can hold gatherings and Powwows, that is a huge step forward. I mean, the Klan doesn't hassle us anymore. But I'm pretty sure some of them are still out there, in one form or another.

For instance, about thirty years after our cross-burning episode, I was working as a building inspector, and I had to check out a house in the woods that belonged to one of the white families that used to be part of the Klan. The man who owned the house, he knew it would be trouble for me to go back there by myself, so he agreed to be there. He was anxious to get his house inspected, and he couldn't afford to have his kinfolk run me off. Well, nobody bothered me because I was with that one guy the whole time, but I had this feeling we were being watched.

Okay, so the Klan is gone, nobody will put up with that anymore. Good riddance. But all you have to do is turn on the TV or pick up a newspaper and you see there are these guys called skinheads today. The people with any color, the skinheads want to kill 'em if they get the chance.

It's too bad that people can't be people without looking at skin color, or where you live, how you talk, things like that. In order to get along with people, you have to almost talk their language, you have to try to understand them. How hard is that?

Why can't we look past our differences and see what we have in common?

It seemed like things were getting better, especially in the 1990s, but now it feels like we're going in reverse. For one thing, leadership is missing—altogether missing. Some of the white people who head our government today are a throwback to the white people who came here a long time ago, in my opinion. They take what they want, they lie to everyone including themselves about their motives. And they put themselves on a pedestal.

Well, you can tell everything you need to know about people by their actions. All you have to do is look at how the government handled Hurricane Katrina to see what kind of people are running our country. We can put a man on the moon but we can't get black people out of New Orleans to higher ground?

I wish somebody would put me in charge of FEMA. I'd love to tackle that. I'd fix things up good.

It's like this war in Iraq. If it were up to me, we wouldn't be there. Lenape women would never have approved that one. It didn't make any sense to go there! All these young soldiers doing their best, in some cases losing their lives, in other cases being wounded or scarred for life. It breaks your heart! And all the innocent people in Iraq getting killed. For what? Supposedly, to end terrorism. But it's made things worse.

My generation fought World War II. We did what we had to do. Sometimes they call us "the greatest generation." I'm not sure that's correct. I don't know why we would be the "greatest." I think the young people in America today would do the same under similar circumstances. I think they have what it takes.

Modern Life

It's not just what we're doing overseas, though. You look around today, you wonder if people in power really value old people and little children here at home. You look at the budget, the way the government spends money. That's the first thing they cut, money for old people and little children. I wish I was running things because I would straighten that out right away. It's the exact opposite of the Indian way, because we believe in putting Elders and children first. Even when we gather to eat, Elders are lined up first. Then the mothers with small children. If you're young and healthy, you've got to wait your turn. Hope you're not too hungry. Ha!

I wish we could get somebody again like Franklin Roosevelt, a president who believed that all people have potential. That is what makes America great—don't cut off people at the knees, but give everybody a chance to rise to the top.

But it seems to me that working people are really getting hurt and no one cares. Taxes are high, expenses are high. Housing and gasoline cost a fortune. Everything does! Heck, it even costs a lot of money to get yourself buried when you die! It's not like the old days when they dug a hole and put you in the ground and left you there. No, today you got to have all this rigmarole, casket and all that. It's the law! You're stuck with it! It's not even cheap to die anymore. Ha! I think that's kind of funny.

Sometimes all you can do is laugh.

24

The Indian population, we have our way of doing things and it's been handed down, handed down, handed down. So maybe we don't all have brand-new cars, and maybe we don't all have great big houses. But if you're concerned about the future, about future generations, you would see that those things are not important anyway.

I read in the paper or see on television that there are all these young people struggling to live a certain way. They need to think for themselves, stop listening to advertising that makes them feel bad, left out.

I think you have to be comfortable with yourself to have a happy life. You have to say, "This is what's important to me. I'm not going to 'buy' into that. I don't need a huge house. I'd rather spend more time with my family. I'd rather do more for my community."

If people changed their priorities and slowed down a bit, they would learn that it's very pleasant to lead a simple life. If you're in a rush, you miss all the things that are worthwhile.

Suppose you see somebody in a store and that person's having a hard time getting a cart around, something like that. Maybe they're sick or old, or maybe it's a pregnant lady. So you stop and ask, "Can I help you?" If they refuse, at least you feel good that you asked. But if they say, "Yes, I'd like some help," that's even better because you get to make somebody's day. Making someone else happy, even if it's just a little bit, is the key to being content. People don't necessarily know how to do this. They have to learn it from somebody, by example.

I wish we could let kids be kids again. Stop protecting them half to death. Look at these kids! They're so fat! And it's terrible, because they're only little kids and they might have diabetes or high blood pressure. Send them outside to play. Let them climb trees and chase butterflies.

Maybe kids wouldn't need drugs if somebody taught them that when they're frustrated or upset, there are other ways to deal with those feelings. If you pull a few weeds in the garden you can say, "Hey, that's a little bit that I've done today, besides what I had planned to do." So, you're helping yourself by going out and messing in the garden. Or you can sit out there and have a glass of ice tea, sit and just listen to the birds sing. A squirrel might go across the yard. These kinds of things are what calm us down. Be observant. Learn to be still and quiet.

Your body can cure itself if you help it. If you don't, or if you do things to your body that are detrimental, then eventually that part's going to take over.

I'm talking about minor problems of the body and mind. Things like cancer, that's a different story. Then you go to the doctor. I mean stress-related things, problems that are in your power to correct.

You don't have to take a whole lot of medicine and knock yourself out to achieve these things. When you do something like weed your garden, or just sit outdoors and breathe, a lot of things will fall into place. You can get rid of that feeling you've got, that closed-in feeling, like somebody's trying to take something away from you and you don't know how to counteract it. All of a sudden you have that feeling of, "Oh, now I realize why I couldn't understand before."

If necessary, if something's really bothering you, that's when you go to somebody and ask for help. That's what friends are for. That's what Elders are for.

Interacting with other people—as long as they aren't the kind that gossip and tell tales—is very therapeutic. All my life, people have come to me for advice, and I really don't know why. It's something anyone can do. I have a relative who called me the other day and she says, "Cousin Marion, I always looked up to you. Anytime I ever asked you a question you was always able to answer it." And I don't even remember doing it!

If I could say one thing to parents today, it would be, "Allow your children to be independent." I hear about kids who go off to college who can't wash their own clothes, get themselves up in the morning in time to get to class, and so on.

And if there was one gadget I could wipe off the face of the earth, it would be these doggone cell phones. Oh, I hate those darned things. Don't like them for love nor money. Those people who are driving and talking on 'em, they're not concentrating on what they're doing. And wherever you go, it seems like somebody's always holding one up to their ear, and talking, talking, talking.

Modern Life

Telephones, in general, are an example of something good that has been totally ruined. Lord help you if you want to make a simple phone call today to a bank or whatnot. Who's on the other end? Nobody, that's who! It's a machine! Now, how crazy is that? They tell you, "If you want to do thus and so, push button one. If you want to do such-and-such, push two. If you want to talk to somebody or leave a message, push three." When I get one of those machines, I hang up. I'm not talking to any machine. I'm a person, I want to be treated like a person.

Sometimes I think younger folks don't have a clue what I'm talking about, anyway. I know I use some old-time expressions. They probably think, "That old lady doesn't have any sense."

Well, I'm an old-fashioned kind of gal, and I use expressions that I grew up with. The other day, someone called me long distance and during the conversation, they asked me what the weather was like here. And I said, "Oh, we got ourselves a mackerel sky." And they said, "What on earth are you talking about?" And I said, "Mackerel, you know, like the fish." And they said, "The sky looks like a fish?!"

I had to explain that the clouds are striated, or striped, just like a mackerel's scales. It means the weather is changing.

Well, I happen to like that expression, so I've decided I'm going to continue using it, anyway. Even if I'm the last person on earth who knows what it means. Why should I change?

PART XI

The Last Word

MARION STRONG MEDICINE has arrived early and parked her 1995 Oldsmobile in the grass under a shade tree on the tribe's rural property. It is Sunday afternoon of the fall Spiritual Gathering. It has been six months since her husband died.

The first structure on the property, a pole barn, has been built, and everyone is in the mood to celebrate. At last there is a permanent shelter, in case of inclement weather, on the sprawling property.

Strong Medicine visits with other Elders. The ceremony in the Sacred Circle has been over for an hour, and it's time to eat. Elders are supposed to eat first, followed by mothers and small children, but she is too involved with amusing her youngest great-grandson, Marcus, to notice. She is sitting on a folding chair, hanging on to the toddler's sweatshirt as he tries to bolt. Finally, he gives up and climbs on her lap. He stares into her face, studying it. They are fixated on each other despite the hubbub around them.

An old man—a classmate from high school, it turns out—spoils the moment. He sneaks up behind Strong Medicine and squeezes her shoulders playfully. Her hand juts up and she pops him lightly in the face with her fist. "Go away!" she says.

"I never did like men sneaking up on me," she says under her breath. The toddler pulls her hair and she laughs. She kisses his little hands, and a smile instantly transforms his face from grumpy to cherubic. He turns and tries to kiss his great-grandma.

The Chief walks by. He is in one of his cantankerous moods. "If you think I'm the most powerful person in the tribe, you're wrong," he says loudly. "It's not me. It's Mom!"

"Oh, watch your mouth," she says, and tries to swat him on the rear.

The Chief pulls up a chair and sits down. He clearly loves his mother. To everyone else at the table, he says, "Mom is modest, and she won't take any credit, but we were lucky to have an Elder I could go to, to sign on the incorporation papers back in seventy-eight."

It's the last outdoor gathering of the year. Soon, winter will arrive. Back at her bungalow later that evening, the mood is more somber. She frets about this winter's heating bills. There are cracks in the walls and the floor of her bungalow which, she believes, is healthy most of the year, for it allows air to circulate. She is worried that the cold drafts may be harmful to her aging bones—and her pocketbook.

But the winter passes with only one significant snowstorm. This she finds deeply troubling, far more worrisome than high energy bills or aching joints. In late February, a warm spell arrives on the East Coast and, while most people rush outside to celebrate the unseasonable warmth, Marion

The Last Word

Strong Medicine stands on her porch, brooding. She remembers winters when the snow covered porches in this area. This is not normal, she says. It's not right. But who is going to listen to an old Indian lady, she wonders.

Someone wrote a letter to the editor of the *New York Times* saying global warming should be renamed "global heating" to reflect the gravity of the situation. When told of this, she smiles in agreement.

Her birthday, April 25, arrives. She is eighty-four years old. It is a beautiful day, and the highest priority of the day is lunch in nearby Millville, followed by a stroll around the yard of her bungalow to see which weeds and other wild plants have decided to make an appearance. The roads to and from her bungalow are blocked occasionally by tractors and other slow-moving farm equipment, but we don't mind. We're on Indian time.

It had been the driest winter on record and spring seemed doomed to being a shadow of itself, but then, three days before Strong Medicine's birthday, the skies had let loose. For three days, it rained in Biblical proportions.

"Lord have mercy!" Strong Medicine cries as we walk randomly around the front yard. In a few hours' time, a bumper crop of chickweed—her favorite plant—has popped up from the ground. In fact, it covers most of the front yard, as if someone has thrown down an enormous quilt while we were gone to lunch.

This is delightful news, a birthday present, it seems, from Mother Nature. Strong Medicine will have more than enough chickweed to make her special healing salve. At the suggestion that perhaps she should patent the recipe and sell it, she shakes her head vigorously. "No," she says, "I am not interested in the money. I want to make my salve for my family only."

She is especially happy to find, alongside the bungalow in the shade, a larger type of chickweed that she prefers. In some years, it doesn't grow at all. She looks for plantain and finds only one lonely little plant, but it's still early in the season. She breaks off a few low, renegade branches of a wild strawberry bush and carries them into the bungalow for their scent.

The day draws to a close. She waves good-bye from the porch, then suddenly signals to wait a moment. She disappears into the bungalow for what seems like a long time. Suddenly, there she is again, back out on the porch, then, her familiar long stride. There is something in her hand—the remaining bottle of last year's chickweed salve. "Take it," she says. "Use it sparingly. I don't know how much longer I'll be able to make it."

25

I like to poke around in my yard, collect my weeds, and make concoctions from them. I learned this from my aunts and my mother, and they learned it from their mother. And so on.

I don't know how much longer I will be able to do it. I'm old now, and I have less energy. I will keep doing it as long as I can—and as long as the plants keep coming up every spring.

Some of the plants are gone now. When I think about all the things that used to be out here, where they got houses now, it makes me sad. Things have been destroyed. There used to be a lot of marsh, a lot more water. You had the prettiest plants, like ferns and lilies—oh, the lilies were all different colors, yellow, orange, all wild. Something you could really enjoy. You didn't bring 'em home because they needed to be in water. You just admired them right where they were.

Now there are some houses there and the folks wonder why they have flooding. Ha! They don't know that the waterline comes up 'cause there's a tributary that comes under the road. It goes down toward Bridgeton, and they've got it piped somewhere down that way. It goes on over to another tributary, and then to the Cohansey River. And then to the Delaware Bay.

My bungalow is up on a hill, so I don't get flooding. But

there might have been water up here, too. Way back when Wilbur's uncle used to live across the street—him and his wife used to farm back there—there was a lot of stones, all kinds of stones back there. So I think there was water running in through there, too.

It's not there anymore.

This was a dirt road until the 1950s or maybe the '60s. I don't remember when they paved it. When it was dirt, there used to be all kinds of wild plants growing along the edge. Of course, what few cars went by, you'd have a cloud of dust. That was not so great. When I was a kid, and we lived down the road, we had an awful time keeping the house clean. I would dust the front rooms and next thing I know, Mom would open the windows. Sure enough, a few minutes later, that was when a car would go by. Then Mom would walk back in the dining room and see all this dust on the table and say, "Marion, look at all that dust on the table!" Oh, it made me mad.

Well, now the road is paved and the cars and trucks fly by here like there's no tomorrow. I don't know where they think they need to be that's so important. Makes you almost miss the days when it was a dirt road.

One thing that has changed for the better is that the turkeys have come back again. They were almost extinct, hunted to death. Then the government made it illegal to hunt them, and now we have wild turkeys again. It makes you feel good, because they're supposed to be here. They have a right to be here!

I have five turkeys that like to hang around my backyard. They are huge. Tall enough that I can see their heads when they

*walk past my window! When I notice they've come to visit me,
I go from room to room to watch them from the windows.*

*For a while, one was missing, and I got a little worried. I
thought, "Maybe something has happened to him. Or maybe
he's just under the weather." Then one day he reappeared with
the others. Of course, I can't be 100 percent sure it was him.
But I would venture to guess that it was. And I was so happy
to see him again.*

*My granddaughter Ty is very interested in learning how to
make my chickweed salve. It'll heal just about anything. Takes
the pain out, too. If I can't find much chickweed, some years I
use plantain instead—not the tropical kind of plantain, but the
kind that grows around here, in North America. Evidently,
chickweed and plantain have the same properties.*

*Last year we had these teeny-tiny kind of chickweed with a
heart-shaped leaf and a little tiny white flower. You have to be
flexible, and be grateful at whatever Mother Nature gives you.*

*Now, the plantain has two different shapes. The one I see
most often is a long skinny plant with one stem that comes up in
a little bulb. We used to pop the bulbs off and pretend to shoot
'em at each other when we were kids. That kind is a bumblebee
weed, but it's part of the plantain family.*

*Another plant I like to use is tansy. You grind up the yellow
flowers and keep it handy in case you cut yourself. You tap
some of it on the cut and it heals itself.*

*I also love mint. I have several different kinds in my yard. If
you make tea from the leaves, it will help in digestion. It also
helps with insomnia, coughs, and nervousness. The leaves can
be used in the bath, too, to soothe skin.*

Some of the plants I like to eat are weeds. Well, other people call them weeds! They're vegetables as far as I'm concerned. Some Indians are embarrassed to admit they eat this stuff, but I'm not.

Most people look at weeds and first thing you know, they spray something nasty called Roundup on 'em. They want that perfect yard, you know. They need to be educated, because all plants have value. And they don't stop and think that the stuff they spray gets on their clothes, their children, their dog, and everything else. Then, when it rains, that toxic stuff goes somewhere. It gets into the streams and rivers. It gets into the drinking water.

During the Great Depression, back in the thirties, Indians survived by eating weeds. We knew how to get by. I've eaten more weeds in my life than I-don't-know-what. You just wash them and put a little olive oil on it, and it's good. One of the weeds we used to eat—I still do—is called lamb's-quarters. It's sort of a dusty green leaf, with serrated leaves. Another one is poke, which some people call pokeweed or pokeroot. The only part you eat is when the leaves are small.

Poke is also very useful as a way to break a high fever. This is what you do: You take part of the root, and you scrape some of it off with a grater, then add a little vinegar. You heat that up over a fire or low oven. Then, you take an old sheet and tear it up into strips. You put some of the poke on the strips and you wrap them around the sick person's wrists and feet—the bottoms of their feet. I just did that for my grown grandson a few weeks ago, and he felt better in no time.

Another plant you can use for poultices is mullein. It has a dusty green leaf with small yellow flowers that we used to call "Old Man's Flannel."

It's also important to know what not to pick, because there are some poisonous plants. For instance, milkweed is a diuretic and good for asthma but in larger quantities it's poisonous. You also have to be careful with milk thistle. In small quantities the leaves can help with stomach problems, like a lack of appetite. And the seeds can help with spleen, gallstone, and liver problems, or so I was told long ago.

Some people still grow a flowering plant called snowballs, but they probably have no idea that the ones that are deep pink to pale pink can be ground up and used for liver problems. But, again, you better be cautious. Just because it's natural doesn't mean it's safe to use except in tiny amounts.

I don't like to tell people what to take because everyone is different. What I do is take small amounts of individual plants and herbs, dry them, and experiment with them. I take one thing at a time and see if it works for me. You have to give it a chance, maybe try it for a week or two or longer. A lot of people will take too much, or they're impatient and they don't give it enough time. Or they take several things at the same time, which is a bad idea.

I grow some things myself, but you'd be surprised what is growing wild if you look for it. You can use chickory as a replacement for coffee, and one of my favorite flavorings is tarragon.

I'm still trying to figure out how in the world anyone could stand those skunk cabbages. People used to take it for something, but I never did. It smells too bad! And it gets in your system, and then you smell bad. Hey, I'm all for natural ways, but I wouldn't go that far.

A lot of the old-timey ways do work, though, and I prefer to use them. I like to let my body heal itself. I haven't had much exposure to modern medicine. I just don't like the way they try to make you take all these pills today. They got a pill for this, and a pill for that. I don't think those drugs have been tested properly. I'm suspicious. I think the drug companies want to rush the drugs to market. It's all about money.

I don't take much of anything. I don't believe in it. I take one vitamin a day, and a heart pill, and one aspirin for my heart. With my heart pill, my doctor said, "I'm not sure whether to give it to you in eighty milligrams or to give you a higher dose." I said, "Well, how about you give me half a dose?" You can't be too careful with these medicines, if you ask me. Everybody is not made the same, and everybody cannot handle the same thing.

Even the vitamins—sometimes they're not what you think. You think you're taking vitamin E, but it's not the real vitamin E. It's the way they process it.

It's better to get your vitamins and minerals naturally, anyway. Diet is very, very important. A lot of Indian people have diabetes, because we haven't been eating white people's food all that long and I think it just doesn't agree with us. They should skip the white bread altogether. And stop eating at all those fastfood restaurants! Go back to the old ways—corn and beans and squash.

Meat used to be a luxury. Nobody could afford ham or beef very often. We used to eat only what the men would hunt, and that included rabbits, muskrats, and groundhogs. Some of the old-timers in the tribe still make groundhog stew. Not me! Even when I was younger, I wouldn't eat groundhog or muskrat, though Wilbur and the boys did. I prefer fish from the ocean, or the streams, but now you got to worry that there's too much mercury and some other junk in it.

When I was coming up, there were a lot of childhood diseases that people had to contend with. This was before they had vaccines. You got measles, mumps, polio, diphtheria, all kinds of stuff. I had rheumatic fever, which harms your heart, but other than that I've been pretty healthy my whole life.

I worry a little about cancer because it runs in my family. Then again, there's some longevity in my family, too. One of my aunts just died and she was past one hundred years old.

In recent years my only problem has been Lyme disease. I got it from these nasty little deer ticks that seem to be everywhere these days. I hate those darn things. I read that they're all over the United States now, and I just don't understand that. Must be because we're messing with the environment, that's all I can figure, because when I was growing up, and when my boys were little, it wasn't a problem. Never even heard of deer ticks then. You'd go out and play in the grass and you never had a tick on you afterward. We had dog ticks, but they went after the dog, not the people.

When I got Lyme disease, my doctor put me on this strong antibiotic. Well, I don't like antibiotics. I've hardly ever taken them. There was this young couple who had joined my church, and she was a nurse. I told her what I was taking and she said, "Well, make sure you drink at least eight ounces of water with each of those pills." That worried me. So I doubled the amount of water—sixteen ounces. I figured, if it gets hung up some-where in your body, then it's going to stay there and dissolve and you don't know what it's going to do. But it won't be good.

That was ten years ago. Now, if I think I've been bit by a tick, I put black walnut on the spot. I keep it in the cupboard in a dropper bottle. You can make it yourself if you have black walnuts growing in your yard or you can buy it at a health food store.

I hate going to the doctor. I don't go very often, maybe once a year. The last time I went to see him, we had a quarrel. I felt he was talking down to me. So I told him, "Listen, I don't like the way you're talking to me. I think I'm going to leave now." And he tried to talk me out of it, but he couldn't. I'd had enough.

Finally, he said, "Well, when you change your mind, call and make a new appointment, and come back." Frankly, I had already made up my mind that I wasn't coming back. Ever. As I walked down the hallway past the receptionist's desk I said under my breath, "Ha! You know what you can do with your appointment!" All of a sudden I realized there's a lady from my church sitting right there in the waiting room, and she heard me swearing. Wouldn't you just know it?

26

I got to see the way modern medicine is set up for old people when my husband took sick. It's a sin and a shame, the way old people are treated, at least from what I've seen. Sometimes, you've really got to fight to be treated with dignity, and that is wrong!

I wanted Wilbur to come home from the hospital and die the Indian way, with his grandchildren and great-grandchildren around, so they could see him and he could see them, but the system was against that.

This is what happened: Wilbur started having problems two years before he died. He passed out. I think this was August of '03. He kept having spells, so I called the doctor and he told me to bring him in. We went to Delaware, to the veterans hospital, and they gave him some medication. Then they sent him home.

You know, I loved that man but he could drive a person crazy. Wilbur had this habit where he would go out and cut grass on the lawn mower, and he'd go all up in the back field but leave the side yards unmowed. Well, what's the sense in that? But he got to the point where he would go out to mow the lawn and first thing I know he's back to the house and hadn't cut any grass. He said he didn't feel like doing it. This was not a good sign.

So we took him back to the veterans hospital in Delaware. My brother-in-law, Margaret's husband, did the driving. This time the doctors decided to keep him. They monitored him for five days and nights. And then they sent him home with a change in medication.

Well, he was doing pretty good. He wasn't like his old self, but we were managing. Some days he'd get dressed and say, "Marion, I feel like going for a ride." So I'd say, "Okay, where do you want to go?" This one time he wanted to go to Wildwood, to the ocean. I was a little surprised because that's kind of far and I said, "Are you sure that's where you want to go?" Then he thought about it and said, "No. Let's go down to Margaret's." Other times, I'd just ride him around through the countryside and get an ice-cream cone or something. And then we would sit there for a while. Maybe we'd talk, maybe we wouldn't. When you've known somebody that long, you don't have to talk.

Then one day when we were getting gas in the car, he said he was feeling poorly, and I noticed his speech was slurred. So back we went to the hospital in Delaware. I forget how long he was there that time, but when they were done with him, they sent him to a nursing home.

That nursing home made me crazy. I'm sure they're not all like that, but this place was awful. And I had researched it, and it was supposed to be good.

Wilbur was brought to the nursing home somewhere around one o'clock, and by six o'clock, he still hadn't been fed. The doctors had put in a feeding tube while he was in the hospital, and he had to be fed through the tube.

So, I kept asking the girl, "When are you going to feed him?" They kept ignoring me. Oh, I raised Cain! I was mad! And I refused to leave until they hooked him up. I didn't trust them to do it if I had gone home.

He wasn't in the nursing home long before he got worse, and he was taken to a hospital nearby. This particular hospital, it was cold. There was a draft coming from the window because the place wasn't built right. And they had the door to the hall-way open all the time, so there was this cold air rushing through the room.

Everybody in the place seemed to be doped up. It was like they were all in a coma. One time, Wilbur's sister Margaret went to see him and she left a note because he was sleeping. When I got there, hours later, he was still sleeping.

I don't know why they did this to Wilbur, but they had him so he was hanging up, sitting almost upright. But he wasn't conscious, he was asleep from all the drugs they give 'em, and so his head was hanging down. I tried to get him situated so he would be more comfortable. I couldn't leave him hanging there like that. When I pulled off the sheets, come to find out they had his feet fastened down. Strapped down!

I found the staff and I told them, "You'd better unfasten his feet right now. I don't want those things on his feet! And I don't want him hanging there like that!"

This was in a cardiac care unit. This nurse or social worker came to talk to me. Frankly, I couldn't tell who I was talking to, because they don't wear different uniforms like *they used to in the old days. You can't tell a doctor from an orderly anymore. Maybe they have it written on their little name tag, but, hey, when you're old, you can't always read those little name tags.*

Anyway, she asked me what I wanted to do and I told her that I want my husband home. I said, "Home! Not in a hospital. Not in a nursing home! Home!" So, she went and had a little confab with some of her people.

But nobody told me anything. So I found her and I asked her, "How soon are you going to be ready for him to come home?" She said, "Well, I have to get things together." Well, that was fine. So I gave them some time. But then I began to get this feeling that maybe they were avoiding me.

So one day I went looking for her all over the hospital. I found her office. And I stood in the doorway and I said, "Have you made arrangements for my husband to come home?" She said, "No." Finally, she says, "Look, Mrs. Gould, I think you're too old to take care of your husband at home."

I said, "What?! You don't know who you're messing with here. I'm not too old to take care of my husband! Besides, I've got two sons. I've got granddaughters. I got cousins across the street. I've got a whole tribe of people I can call on. If I need help, I'll get help."

But she says, "Mrs. Gould, I don't want you to strain yourself." And I said, "Don't worry about me. Worry about my husband! I want him in the house. I want his grandchildren and great-grandchildren to come to the house and visit him without somebody saying, 'You can't have but two people at the same time.' Because I don't care if it's a whole house full."

She said, "But you're going to hurt yourself." And I said, "I can take care of myself!"

Oh, we had quite a ruckus. I was on the warpath! That did the job, though. So the next day they brought him home. And sure enough, people came out of the woodwork and helped me. That is part of the Indian way.

I had everything all set up. The physical therapist came and worked on his arms and legs. I kept him clean. And I put that liquid food into the tube in his belly. I did other things to help him so that eventually he tried to eat. That is what he wanted. He got frustrated, he got mad sometimes, but I'll tell you one thing: He was conscious. He was talking again. And he felt like a human being again.

I am not saying that all hospitals or nursing homes are like the ones I dealt with. It probably depends how they are run, how much staff they have, and so on. I would even venture to guess that there are times when it's better for a patient to be in the hospital or a nursing home, rather than at home. But in our situation, I think bringing him home was the right thing to do. And I know it's what he wanted.

I'm not saying it was easy. We set up a hospital bed in the living room. I would go to sleep in the bedroom, and sometimes he would come in there and he would go to bed with me. First thing you know, I would wake up and he'd be gone. Sometimes he'd be calling for me from the other room. I would come out to the living room and he might be in the recliner, or he might be in the hospital bed, but he'd have the covers off the bed, he'd have a quilt here, he'd have his bathrobe over there, he had something thrown over here. I'd say, "Lord, have mercy." I have no *idea why he did that but I've seen other people do that when they're really ill.*

And I'd ask him, "Do you want me to help you get dressed again?" So he'd let me help him and invariably he'd come back in the bedroom with me. But first thing you know, I hear him making noises. And I'd turn the light on and I'd ask him, "What's the matter?" He says, "I gotta get out of here. They won't let me stay here." I says, "Who's they?" And he says, "I can't tell you, but they won't let me stay here." I said, "Okay. You want me to go out there with you to the living room?" He says, "Would you?" I says, "Yeah, sure."

I never did find out who he was afraid of. Got to have been Satan. I don't know who else. I know the Lord wouldn't treat him that way. But someone else said maybe he thought the Germans were after him again, that he was reliving the war. Anyhow, I'd get him out here and put him to bed and every-thing. And I'd sit in the chair for a little while, then I'd get tired, go to sleep on the couch, or go back to bed in the bedroom.

Just before he died, he was sitting in the chair and Billy's wife, Yvonne, was here, and called out to me, "Mom, some-thing's wrong with Dad, I can't make him stop." I says, "Stop what?" She says, "He's shaking all over." He had his fists up like he was going to fight. Now, this was two or three days before he passed away.

So I calmed him down a little bit and got him quiet. Yvonne's sister brought her preacher by, and I told Wilbur, "Just keep quiet, we're going to have a prayer for you." I told him, "Let me hold on to you." So I held on to his hands. I said, "Try to be quiet, pastor's going to pray for you." And that happened and everything was okay. Now, this was about five or six o'clock in the afternoon. Then some of the family begin to come. After a while he got settled away and said he wanted to go in the bedroom. So Yvonne and I changed his clothes and washed him down, because he was sweating. Sweating profusely. We got him all cleaned up and everything. The boys were here and they asked me if I was going to take him back to the bed in the living room, and so we did. And I had that wedge cushion that I bought for him and he never wanted to use. I put that behind him so he could lean on it, because he was beginning to rattle. You could hear there was something in his chest, his throat. I'd heard the rattle before in others so I knew basically what it was.

The next day, we went basically through the same thing. He was rattling but it wasn't quite like it was the night before, because I was awake half the time. Yvonne and I decided to clean him up again and by this time, family had started to come again. I went across the street for a minute to his cousin's house, and somebody called an ambulance. They were going to take him to the hospital. But I said, "Good God, leave him be!"

It was after dark when he went. It was sometime between eight and nine o'clock that night. One of my nieces is a nurse, and she was here, and she told me, "Aunt Marion, you better check his blood pressure again." She was using a stethoscope, and I had this blood pressure machine.

I sat up there and watched that thing go from way up here all the way down. His blood pressure was falling way, way down. I was holding his hand, and somebody said something, and I turned to answer them when I heard this noise. And that was it.

It felt like half of me went with him. I loved that man since the first time I saw him, when I was fourteen years old.

These being modern times, somebody remembered that we had to call the police. Can't die at home anymore without doing that. They have to make sure nobody had poisoned him or anything like that. Well, they sent this great big tall policeman. Since we live outside of Bridgeton, it was a state trooper. He was as nice as he could be. He did his job fine. Filled out the paperwork, asked questions, took all of Wilbur's medicine, and stood there and counted it. Left us alone as much as he could.

At least I succeeded in having Wilbur die at home. It was just like the old days, when people had their kinfolk around them. There wasn't a square inch in that room, in the whole house, or on the porch, that somebody wasn't standing or sitting. That's the Indian way, and I'm grateful that I was able to do that for Wilbur.

27

I have been taking care of people my whole life. My little brother and sister, when we were coming up. My own boys. My mother, when she took sick. My father and father-in-law, when they got old. My youngest son. And then Wilbur.

It's a little strange, at this point in my life. I don't have to worry about anyone else. Sometimes it feels good, like I'm free of responsibilities. Other times I feel a little lost. It is hard growing older, and outliving people you love. It makes you feel lonely, but I love being alive, and I'm not going to ruin whatever time I got left by complaining.

The first few months after Wilbur died, it seemed like I spent all my time straightening out paperwork. There were all the medical bills, and all kinds of things to take care of. I had to go to the Social Security office, and the bank, and all that kind of stuff. Have his name taken off of documents. I don't know why, but I couldn't throw out his driver's license. I carry it with me in my wallet, next to mine.

At first I tried to think of things as they were, and forget about the passing and all, and just stay busy, but it started to hit me more and more that he was gone, he had gone to the Lord, to the Creator, and I was living by myself for the first time in my entire life. Of course, Billy lives right next door and he pops in and out of here, and Mark stops by when he can. When I had the flu, Mark came over here and cooked for me. My granddaughter Ty calls me almost every day, and she pops in with the kids—she has five. And my sister, Dianne, lives in Vineland. And so on.

With Billy living right next door, I feel like I got to check in with him whenever I go out, ever since Wilbur died. I don't really like that. I don't think I should have to tell Billy what I'm doing all the time, where I'm going, and what I'm up to. It annoys me a little bit, even though, at the same time, I am grateful.

Yesterday, Billy and his wife came in the back door. They said, "Mom, are you all right? We're just checking on you." They sat down and we talked for a while. It's part of the Indian way to look after your Elders, but I'm of two minds about it, because they're both still working, they've got lives of their own, and I don't want them fretting over me.

Now, Mark took me to the eye doctor the other day. I still drive, but when you get your eyes examined they make your vision all blurry and I didn't want to drive home like that. So Mark took me. When I came out of the examining room, I had to laugh, 'cause Mark was sitting in the waiting room, sound asleep. I said, "Hey, you, you're turning into an old man, falling asleep like that!" It's something, watching your children get older. Both my sons are in their sixties now.

A long time ago I told them something they've never forgotten. I said that when I'm gone, I didn't want them visiting my grave all the time and leaving flowers there. No, I'd rather they

Marion "Strong Medicine" Gould in
front of her bungalow, summer 2006.

*move on with their lives. And besides, I'd rather have my flow-
ers now, while I can enjoy them. So ever since I told them that,
my boys bring me flowers.*

*I realize I am lucky to have my family nearby. I miss my
husband very much, but I don't talk about it much. When I'm
sad, I go outside and listen to the sounds of Mother Nature.
Basically, I'm an optimistic person, and I think if you keep trying, there is always a way to dig out of whatever problem you
have.*

"STRONG MEDICINE" SPEAKS

Until the Creator calls me home, I expect to be right here, on this same stretch of road, puttering in my yard, gathering my weeds, and talking to my birds. I've seen some hard times, but I am deeply satisfied with my life. As a matter of fact, I wouldn't change it for anything in this world.

"*Wanishi*" ("Thank You")

Creating this book has been an extraordinary, once-in-a-lifetime journey. I am thankful and honored that the Nanti-coke Lenni-Lenape people allowed me into their lives, especially, of course, the remarkable Elder Marion "Strong Medicine" Gould. Her gift of time, knowledge, and friendship has been life-changing. I am enormously grateful to the Creator for leading me to her.

In typical Lenape style, I must give credit to the Creator, in fact, for all the tools He gave me for this journey: persistence, sensitivity, faith, patience, curiosity, good instincts, respect for others, a strong sense of justice, and all the skills as a listener, interviewer, journalist, author, and photographer that I have accumulated over the years.

From Marion Strong Medicine, I have learned to live the "Indian way." I have "slowed down" and reprioritized my life. Whenever possible, I avoid using a cell phone, a car—even a watch. I have culled some activities that made my life frantic but added little to my overall happiness. While I have always enjoyed nature, I have learned to be more observant, to be still and listen, and to find peace in the gifts of Mother Earth. No matter how busy I am, I make a greater effort to put work aside and spend time with friends and family.

"Wanishi" ("Thank You")

There are so many people to acknowledge that I hardly know where to begin. This book would not exist without the trust and faith bestowed upon me by Chief Mark "Quiet Hawk" Gould. In time, he extended the hand of friendship not only to me but to my husband, Blair (who, as always, shared this journey with me).

My editor at Atria Books, Malaika Adero, loved this project from day one, as did my literary agent, Mel Berger of the William Morris Agency. Their respect for Strong Medicine and eagerness to see this book published helped give me the tenacity and dedication to see it through. Norman Brokaw, chairman of the board of the William Morris Agency, offered me personal encouragement, as always.

I am also very grateful to my publishers: Jack Romanos, former president and chief executive officer of Simon & Schuster; Carolyn K. Reidy, president and chief executive officer of Simon & Schuster; Judith Curr, executive vice president and publisher of the Simon & Schuster imprint Atria Books; and Gary Urda, deputy publisher of Atria Books.

I wish, also, to thank Malaika Adero's editorial team at Atria Books, including Krishan Trotman, associate editor; Nicholas Sneed, associate; and Isolde Sauer, production editor.

I am enormously grateful to Tina "Little Wild Flower" Pierce Fragoso, the tribal historian (and now a member of the Tribal Council) who was the first person I spoke to back in 2004, when I contacted the tribe. I must, of course, thank the Tribal Council, composed (in late 2004) of Mark Gould, Lewis Pierce, Roberta Flores, Mark Webster, Patricia Rossello, Herbert "Butch" Pierce, Herbert "Uncle Herbie" Pierce, John Norwood, and Urie Ridgeway. Elders who permitted me to interview them include Mary "Spreading Eagle Wings" Ward,

"Wanishi" ("Thank You")

Belford "Iron Eagle" Cuff, Ruth Pierce, and the remarkable Duke and Terp, among others.

I should also thank my own "Elders"—my parents, Dorothy and Lee H. Hill Jr. I am grateful to my dad for researching the family history of our ancestors, the Applegate/Stout/Irons family. I credit my mom with fostering in me an independent spirit.

I appreciate the support of my siblings: my brother Lee H. Hill III; my sister, Helen Hill Kotzky; and my brother Dr. Jonathan D. Hill, who, as an anthropologist, was able to provide helpful feedback and suggestions. (He is past chair of the Department of Anthropology, Southern Illinois University at Carbondale, and coeditor of the journal *Identities*.)

Three others deserve special recognition: John R. Firestone, of Pavia & Harcourt, who is my longtime publishing attorney and a personal friend; Brigit M. Kotzky, my summer intern in 2005 and 2006; and Kim M. Kotzky, my summer intern in 2007.

Several people provided technical advice and consultation: Charles Burrus, who encouraged me to buy a Canon EOS 20D, which I used to take the photographs in this book; and Charles Foster, who made some excellent suggestions regarding digital video.

I would also like to thank Mollie Hoben and Glenda Martin at the BookWomen Center for Feminist Reading, Minnesota Women's Press, Inc. (www.womenspress.com). Located in St. Paul, the center publishes BookWomen, a national newsletter for readers of books by and about women, and which is a source of inspiration for me.

Last but not least, I wish to thank my writers' group, the Atomic Engineers, who have been cheering me on every step of the way (especially Audrey Vernick, who read an early draft of this manuscript). The other members are Pat Olsen, Janet Mazur, Gwen Moran, Jo Kadlecek, Marlene Satter, Catherine Scheader, Lillian Africano, and Caren Chesler.

For more information about the Nanticoke Lenni-Lenape Indians, or to join Friends of the Nanticoke Lenni-Lenape Indians, visit www.nanticoke-lenape.info on the Internet or write to Friends of the Nanticoke Lenni-Lenape Indians, P.O. Box 132, 18 E. Commerce St., Bridgeton, NJ 08302.

To everyone involved in this project, *"Wanishi!"* ("Thank you!")

Lenape Languages:
A Brief Primer

Contributed by John "Smiling Thunderbear" Norwood, Tribal Council member, Nanticoke Lenni-Lenape Indians

Lenape is considered by many linguists to be the root Algonquin/Algonkian (or Algic) tongue. The Lenape dialects at the outset of European contact included Munsee, Unami (Northern and Southern), and Unalachtigo. Work is being done to retain or revive both Munsee and Southern Unami (Modern Unami).

Northern Unami (mostly recorded by Moravian missionaries with some admixture of Southern Unami and Munsee vocabulary in a form called "Mission Lenape") was well preserved by Moravian missionaries and is an intermediate dialect linguistically between the two being revived today, but not in common use for more than 150 years. Unalachtigo merged into Southern Unami and little is known about it as a separate dialect today.

Lenape Languages: A Brief Primer

Nanticoke, a separate language, was not as well preserved as the Munsee or Unami dialects, but is related to Lenape. Spelling systems have varied over time and between dialects; however, in spite of varied spelling, many words are similarly pronounced.

The word for "Creator," which literally means "He who creates us by thought," is *Gischellemelank* or *Gischelemukwenk* in Mission Lenape/Northern Unami; *Kishelemukonk* in Southern Unami; and *Kiisheelumukweengw* in Munsee.

"Mother" is *Gahowees* or *Guka* (Mamma) in Mission Lenape/Northern Unami; *Ana* or *Nkahes* (my mother) in Southern Unami; *Nguk* (my mother) in Munsee; and *Nicque* in Nanticoke.

"Father" is *Nocha* in Mission Lenape/Northern Unami; *Nuxa* in Southern Unami; *Noox* in Munsee; and *Nowoze* (my father) in Nanticoke.

The word for "husband" or "wife" is *Wikimak* or *Witawe-mak* in Mission Lenape/Northern Unami; *Wicheochi* in Southern Unami; *Wiitaweemak* in Munsee; and *Nups-soh-soh* or *Nee-eeswah* in Nanticoke.

The word for "Chief" is *Sakima* or *Wayauwe* in Mission Lenape/Northern Unami; *Sakima* in Southern Unami; and *Kihkay* in Munsee.

"Yes" is *bischi* or *bischik* in Mission Lenape/Northern Unami; *pishi* or *e-e* in Southern Unami; *pi ish* in Munsee; and *a-a-mch* in Nanticoke.

The word for "no" is *atta* or *matta* in Mission Lenape/Northern Unami; *ku* or *ku ta* in Southern Unami; *ma h* in Munsee; and *mattah* in Nanticoke.

Lenape Languages: A Brief Primer

"Thanks" is *anischi* in Mission Lenape/Northern Unami; *wanishi* in Southern Unami; and *anushiik* in Munsee.

Common phrases in Mission Lenape/Northern Unami include: *He!* ("Hello!"); *Kwangomel!* ("I greet you!"); *Unechtgo-Lenni Lenape n'hackey* ("I am Nanticoke Lenni-Lenape"); *Lappitsch knewel* ("I will see you again"); and *Wawullamallessil* ("Fare thee well continually").

Lenape Myths: A Sampling

Author's note: The Lenape tradition of storytelling is an oral one. For hundreds of years, however, anthropologists, historians, and Christian missionaries have been writing down Lenape myths. They appear in many texts, but the most comprehensive guide to date is Mythology of the Lenape *by John Bierhorst. These are excerpts of several of them; names and dates of the person who recorded them are given in the Notes section.*

Turtle Island
Turtle, or tortoise, as the origin of earth.

At first there was only water; the tortoise raised its back, water ran off, and the earth became dry. A tree grew up in the middle of the earth; the first man sprouted from the tree's root, the first woman from the tip of the tree as it bent over and touched the earth.

Woman Who Fell from the Sky
A different Lenape creation myth points to woman as the first human being on earth. Here is a synopsis of one version.

In the sky world, where there was a sunlike body called great cornstalk, a woman had a child; she was sick; she thought

257

she could be cured if the cornstalk could be pulled up. When it was pulled, there was total darkness. Vexed, the people threw the woman and her child down the hole where the cornstalk had been. The two were caught on the backs of hawks, who lowered them to the back of a turtle. A loon dived in the sea and brought back earth.

Dog Stories

Dogs must be treated with respect because they guard the bridge to the afterworld, the bridge that lies at the fork in the Milky Way.

A dog, to oblige its master, killed a snake and thereafter demanded to be fed at the table.

Wehixamukes, the Trickster

A trickster is a person whose adventures usually turn into mishaps. The Lenape trickster, Wehixamukes, causes great vexation by his literal interpretations.

A boy born with a finger missing (from each hand) grew fast, began to work miracles; he went out with hunters to get bear. The leader told all the men to "put their noses to the ground." The former boy, now trickster, took the instruction literally and buried his head in the ground with his buttocks sticking up. . . . Traveling on, the men see an enemy party and say to each other that they want to "throw them down on the ground." The trickster takes it literally and begins throwing the enemies to the ground. . . . The trickster [when corrected] always says, "Flu! You should have told me straight."

Lenape Myths: A Sampling

Origin of Winter

An old couple living in the north quarreled, and the wife went south; now and then the man relents and pays her a visit, bringing along with him the north wind.

Notes

Introduction

2 *the European explorer Giovanni da Verrazzano:* While it is possible that the Lenape interacted with other Europeans at an earlier date, the encounter with the explorer Giovanni da Verrazzano is described as "the first solid evidence of such a visit," according to Edwin G. Burrows and Mike Wallace in their Pulitzer Prize–winning book, *Gotham,* p. 11. Verrazzano's "Report to Francis I," July 8, 1524, is published in Evan T. Pritchard, *Native New Yorkers.* Note that the City of New York officially misspells the name of the explorer (the "Verrazano-Narrows Bridge"). The correct spelling is "Verrazzano."

3 *Lenape were shot by Hudson's men:* Pritchard, *Native New Yorkers,* p. 140.

3 *Historians now believe:* The Lenape "clearly thought the arrangement temporary and local in nature, if indeed there was any agreement at all." Pritchard, *Native New Yorkers,* p. 150.

4 *"They served as scouts":* Pritchard, *Native New Yorkers,* p. 373.

5 *"No other tribe":* quoted in Colin G. Calloway, *New Worlds for All,* p. 145.

5 *"City of Amnesia":* Pritchard, *Native New Yorkers,* p. 19. "In the heart of the information center of the world, there is a vacuum of information about that center itself, and its early history" (p. 12).

Notes

6 *"The exodus of these real Native New Yorkers"*: Pritchard, *Native New Yorkers*, p. 10.

7 *"The man from Europe"*: quoted in Peter Matthiessen, *In the Spirit of Crazy Horse*, p. 191.

Part I: The Hidden People

17 *sent out west to a reservation*: Several Elders of the tribe stated separately that land was confiscated and members of the tribe sent to western reservations as recently as 1924. Interviews with Elders of the tribe, conducted by author in 2005–2006.

Part II: In the Land of the Ancestors

26 *one anthropologist*: Herbert C. Kraft, *The Lenape*, p. xv.

Part IV: "I Am Sorry to Inform You . . ."

81 *one third of the eligible Indian population served*: Sources include Charles Wilkinson's *Blood Struggle*, p. 103.

82 *received advanced combat training*: Millville Army Air Field Museum, Millville, New Jersey.

Part VI: Changing Times

127 *"all-time low for tribal existence on this continent"*: Wilkinson, *Blood Struggle*, p. xii.

127 *unemployment as high as 90 percent*: Wilkinson, *Blood Struggle*, p. xii.

127 *Indians living on reservations*: Wilkinson, *Blood Struggle*, p. 23.

Part VII: A Woman's World

152 *burial ground known as Black Creek*: The archaeologist who informed the tribe of the township's intentions is listed in news articles as Rick Patterson. The site was designated as historic by Bradley Campbell, commissioner of the New Jersey Department of Environmental Protection. The property was purchased by the state's Green Acres program for

Notes

$804,000. Campbell credited the Nanticoke Lenni-Lenape, National Trust for Historic Preservation, Preservation New Jersey, and the Vernon Civic Association as "instrumental in saving this archaeological gem from development." The dispute was chronicled in the *Newark Star-Ledger* from May 2001 to March 2005.

153 *Burden's Hill Forest:* The four groups that saved eighteen hundred acres of land in the Burden's Hill Forest in southern New Jersey were the New Jersey Conservation Foundation, the New Jersey Green Acres Program, the New Jersey Department of Environmental Protection, and the Natural Lands Trust.

Part VIII: Native Pride

167 *legal papers incorporating:* An account of the tribe's incorporation is included in C. A. Weslager, *The Nanticoke Indians,* p. 255.

168 *at-large members:* The at-large members were Mary Ward, Raymond Ridgeway, Phyllis Gould, Edith Pierce, and Frank Munson. See Weslager, *The Nanticoke Indians,* p. 255.

168 *about 150 people:* Weslager, *The Nanticoke Indians,* p. 256.

168 *"The Indian revival":* Wilkinson, *Blood Struggle,* p. xiv.

170 *"Compared to the clashes":* Russell Bourne, *Gods of War, Gods of Peace,* pp. xiii–xiv.

171 *Heckewelder, an early missionary:* Bourne, *Gods of War, Gods of Peace,* p. 197.

171 *the Lenape express reverence:* Nanticoke Lenni-Lenape 2006 Powwow book, "Uniting All Lenape People."

172 *May the circle:* Song lyrics adaptation of "Will the Circle Be Unbroken" by John "Smiling Thunderbear" Norwood.

Part IX: Full Circle

187 *Her granddaughter Lia Watching Sparrow:* Tyrese and Shannon Gould are Mark Gould's daughters from his first marriage, to Phyllis Gould. Lia Gould is his daughter with his second wife, Gail Gould.

Notes

Lenape Myths: A Sampling

Myths are excerpted with permission from *Mythology of the Lenape: Guide and Texts*, by John Bierhorst (Tucson: University of Arizona Press, 1995).

257 Turtle Island: p. 28; originally in Jasper Danckaerts, *Journal of Jasper Danckaerts, 1679–1680*, ed. B. B. James and J. F. Jameson (New York: Scribner's, 1913).

257 Woman Who Fell from the Sky: p. 34; originally Cass-Trowbridge manuscript, 1821–22, quoted in Charles A. Weslager, *The Delaware Indian Westward Migration* (Wallingford, Pa.: Middle Atlantic Press, 1978).

258 Dog Stories: first story, p. 65; originally in Bruce L. Pearson, *A Grammar of Delaware* (Dewey, Okla.: Touching Leaves Indian Crafts, 1988), and Ph.D. diss., University of California, Berkeley, 1972. Second story, p. 65, originally from Herbert C. Kraft and John T. Kraft, *The Indians of Lenapehoking* (South Orange, N.J.: Seton Hall University Museum, 1985).

258 Wehixamukes, the Trickster: p. 60; originally from Carl F. Voegelin, "Delaware Texts," *International Journal of American Linguistics II*, 1945.

259 Origin of Winter: p. 36; originally from Clara Gowing, "Indian Traditions," ms., p. 4, Kansas State Historical Society, Topeka, circa 1860.

Bibliography

Books

Bierhorst, John. *Mythology of the Lenape: Guide and Texts*. Tucson: University of Arizona Press, 1995.

Bourne, Russell. *Gods of War, Gods of Peace: How the Meeting of Native and Colonial Religions Shaped Early America*. New York: Harcourt, 2002.

Brinton, Daniel G. *The Lenape and Their Legends*. New York: AMS Press, 1969. Reprinted from a copy in the collections of the Brooklyn Public Library, from the edition of 1884 published in Philadelphia.

Burrows, Edwin G., and Mike Wallace. *Gotham: A History of New York City to 1898*. New York: Oxford University Press, 1999.

Calloway, Colin G. *New Worlds for All: Indians, Europeans, and the Remaking of Early America*. Baltimore: Johns Hopkins University Press, 1997.

Erdoes, Richard, and Alfonso Ortiz, eds. *American Indian Myths and Legends*. New York: Pantheon, 1984.

Kraft, Herbert C. *The Lenape: Archaeology, History, and Ethnography*. Newark: New Jersey Historical Society, 1986.

Kraft, Herbert C., and John T. Kraft. *The Indians of Lenapehoking*. South Orange, N.J.: Seton Hall University Museum, 1985.

Matthiessen, Peter. *In the Spirit of Crazy Horse*. New York: Viking, 1983.

Bibliography

Nanticoke Lenni-Lenape Powwow book, "Uniting All Lenape People," 2006.

Pritchard, Evan T. *Native New Yorkers: The Legacy of the Algonquin People of New York*. Tulsa, Okla.: Council Oak Books, 2002.

Speck, Frank G. *The Nanticoke Community of Delaware*. New York: AMS Press, 1981. Reprint of 1915 edition published by the Museum of the American Indian, Heye Foundation, New York.

Weslager, C. A. *The Delaware Indians: A History*. New Brunswick, N.J.: Rutgers University Press, 1972. Fifth paper printing, 2003.

Weslager, C. A. *Delaware's Buried Past: A Story of Archaeological Adventure*. University of Pennsylvania Press, 1944. New Brunswick, N.J.: Rutgers University Press, 1968.

Weslager, C. A. *The Nanticoke Indians: Past and Present*. Newark: University of Delaware Press, 1983 (with Associated University Presses of London and Toronto).

Wilkinson, Charles. *Blood Struggle: The Rise of Modern Indian Nations*. New York: Norton, 2005.

Research Institutions

Museum of the City of New York

National Museum of the American Indian (NMAI), Washington, D.C., and New York

New York Public Library

Ocean County Historical Society, Toms River, New Jersey

Rutgers, the State University of New Jersey

Credits and Permissions

To Contact Amy Hill Hearth

Readers who wish to contact the author may do so by visiting www.amyhillhearth.com. A Peabody Award–winning writer whose first book was the *New York Times* bestseller *Having Our Say: The Delany Sisters' First 100 Years*, Ms. Hearth is an oral history specialist. She has been a guest lecturer and visiting author at book clubs, libraries, and academic institutions on topics that include women's history, anthropology, aging, sociology, journalism, and American studies. Ms. Hearth credits her interest in telling the stories of older women to her grandmother, who lived to be 101 years old.

Marion "Strong Medicine" Gould and Amy Hill Hearth.

Printed in the United States
By Bookmasters